marie claire

Outfit 911

marie claire
Outfit 911

Fabulous Fixes for Every Fashion Emergency

Joyce Corrigan

HEARST BOOKS
New York

Introduction by Joanna Coles............ 6

Foreword by Nina Garcia.................. 8

CHAPTER ONE
Dressing for a Job Interview 10

CHAPTER TWO
Dressing for Day to Night 32

CHAPTER THREE
Dressing for a Date 50

CHAPTER FOUR
Dressing for Cool Cocktail Parties
and Black Tie 68

CHAPTER FIVE
Dressing for Clubs and Concerts........ 86

CHAPTER SIX
**Dressing for Official
Functions** 106

CHAPTER SEVEN
**Dressing for a City
Weekend** 124

CHAPTER EIGHT
**Dressing for a Country
Weekend** 142

CHAPTER NINE
Dressing for Great Escapes 160

Index 178

Photo Credits 181

Introduction

My fashion default is the sheath dress. It's my go-to and it never fails. Oh, I've tried dresses with ruffles, weird high-waisted Empire numbers that suggested I was channeling a pregnant Jane Austen, dresses with long sleeves and long skirts that made me disappear, dresses from every designer you've ever heard of and some you haven't (and who quickly disappeared themselves), and as my life—all our lives—get more complicated, still I go back to the tailored confidence of the sheath dress. You can dress it up with necklaces and a belt, down with a blazer, sideways with cuffs and cardis and fur vests, and any old heel will do. I have them in black, olive, gray, navy—and as I was wondering to myself for the hundredth time whether I really needed another squid-ink dark blue one, I suddenly realized what I was trying to do: replicate the ease of my school days, when every morning for fifteen years I got up in my English bedroom and put on the same thing—my school uniform. It was, natch, a navy-blue sheath. Weirdly classic and yet ahead of its time for a uniform, it sailed us through math, social science, woodwork, sometimes with a blue flowery blouse underneath, sometimes a white shirt—depending on the season and the school. Of course, I didn't appreciate it then, didn't get what a relief it was to get up in the morning and face the day not worrying about what to wear. Indeed, anxious to declare my independence at college, I quickly dumped any thoughts of a dress and ran headlong into jeans.

Once I started work as a reporter, I notched it up only one rung by slipping into navy Joseph pants and white shirts. When that got dull there was an inevitable flirtation with separates, but who was I kidding? With my sleeveless tanks and pencil skirts, I was merely recreating the sheath to no advantage because it took longer to get dressed. Turns out that after fifteen years of routine, I couldn't outgrow my uniform. So now I embrace it in wool, cotton, silk and spandex because the sheath dress takes me exactly where I want to go. And that's what this book is for, too. You may not yet have your uniform. But no matter where you're going, whatever you're doing, we have you covered. So, go ahead, browse away. And find the uniform that works for you.

Joanna Coles
Editor in Chief

Foreword

Whenever a special occasion comes along—whether it's a wedding or a job interview—there's a sense of excitement that's followed almost immediately by panic. "What am I going to wear?!" we ask. To calm our nerves we go shopping and often come home with a piece of disposable fashion: the dress, shoes or skirt that's worn once and then never again. Looking back at the purchases that end up taking up much needed space in our closet, we wonder, "What was I thinking?"

Here's the thing: You weren't thinking—at least not clearly. As is the case in any emergency situation, a fashion emergency drives us to be impulsive. Our better judgment gets clouded and we begin grabbing at whatever is new and now—even if it's not quite right. In these situations, it's important to have a lifeline.

Enter *Marie Claire Outfit 911* to help you not only assess the occasion but take you step-by-step through building a wardrobe with long-term staying power. You see, crafting your look isn't a sprint, it's a marathon. With the right training and wise investments you'll always finish first. On your marks, get set, go.

Nina Garcia
Fashion Director

CHAPTER ONE

Dressing for…

a Job Interview

The Interview Look

WHO CAN AFFORD to be forgettable in a competitive work environment? Alongside your stellar resume, your interview look helps a potential employer figure you out: how you see yourself and how well you'd fit into the organization. So, no, it's not the day to get crazy-creative with clothes or accessories that might distract from your personality and professional skills. Dressing in an urbane, classic style—like coloring within the lines—signals your grasp of the notion that discipline and excellence have their place. (Instant bonus points with a potential employer.) Consider an exquisitely tailored suit, a pair of polished pumps or Oxfords and a structured leather handbag as money in the bank.

> **"The road to success is always under construction."**
>
> LILY TOMLIN

PLAYLIST »

Clothing and accessory classics that upgrade your curriculum vitae.

1

2

3

■ **Ruffled blouse**

The button-down style says business, the flourish of fabric signals feminine poise and polish. Consider the ruffle an accessory to exec chic. **(1)**

■ **Classic skirt suit**

A slim black or navy suit might very well usher you into the corner office. **(2)**

■ **Embellished jacket**

Equally right for a pencil skirt or precision-cut pants, a jacket enhanced with precious textures, eye-catching details and shiny buttons won't go unnoticed by HR. **(3)**

4

■ **Structured bag**

No longer just a guy thing, the briefcase takes on a top handle, shiny fixtures and a slimmer silhouette. An attaché you'll grow attached to. **(4)**

5

■ **Pumps**

No matter your natural height, walk tall in the office in a pair of sensationally spirited pumps and you'll give a peak performance. **(5)**

■ **Power watch**

Face to face with a boss-to-be, you'll show your good taste and impeccable timing. **(6)**

6

Corporate or creative?
If you're applying for a government job or at a financial firm like Goldman Sachs, you wouldn't swap outfits with someone interviewing at Google. For more buttoned-down businesses go with traditional matching skirt suits (above and opposite, center) while edgy creative firms will applaud a more progressive approach like pant suits with cropped or fur-trimmed sleeved jackets (opposite, left and far right).

The New Power Suit

Menswear chic breaks out of business-as-usual with sassy suits.

WE MAY BE LIVING in an era of rule-breaking, but here's one not to break: wearing a suit to an interview. A suit—where top and bottom go together—sends a message that *you're* together. That you're ready to start work right then and there. Think of those temporarily unemployed Wall Streeters who still don their pinstripes every day; their effort speaks volumes about dressing for their next dream job. The good news: Business suits have evolved along with modern women. Whether pantsuits or skirt suits, they're confident, curvy and fierce—and now available in a plethora of sleek, stretchy, comfortable fabrics. In short, survival of the fittest.

> "FIND OUT HOW THE EXECS DRESS AT THE FIRM WHERE YOU'RE APPLYING. CALL PEOPLE YOU KNOW. CHECK THEIR WEBSITE FOR TEAM PHOTOS."—Zanna Roberts Rassi, Senior Fashion Editor, *Marie Claire*

Isn't it Iconic?

THOROUGHLY MODERN heroines in menswear have been in Hollywood's spotlight ever since the movies have starred women who mean business. Leading ladies from Kate Hepburn in *Woman of the Year* to Audrey Tatou as the incomparable Chanel knew that in order to cut it with the big boys, they had to present themselves as alpha females long before the nickname was coined. That's where a shapely precision cut suit in a power combo of black, white or gray comes in. (OK, Reese Witherspoon's Elle Woods rethinks this in pink in *Legally Blonde*, but you get the idea.) Feminine accents don't try to steal the show, but are small and discreet: soft blouse, pearls, sophisticated pumps, perhaps a fancy button or pussycat bow here and there.

Hollywood and the working girl
Roles that really suited them: (opposite) Audrey Tatou in *Coco Before Chanel*; (left to right) Rosalind Russell in *Girl Friday*; Katharine Hepburn in *Woman of the Year*; Reese Witherspoon in *Legally Blonde*; Angelina Jolie in *Salt*.

17

Pulling it Together

Suits skirt the issue of looking masculine by adding curves.

P OWER TO THE POLISHED! The jacket is your foundation: Find one that's subtly embellished with a perfect, supple fit. If it's too stiff, you'll come off that way, too. A single-breasted jacket is the safest bet, as a double-breasted cut can sag or call attention to an ample chest or tummy. No better examples of power dressing in the spotlight: France's first lady Carla Bruni out and about on official business in a gray menswear pantsuit topped by a bright purple overcoat. Closer to home, First Lady Michelle Obama raised the White House fashion bar by donning bold solid colors offset with a string of big white pearls (watch your back, Barbara Bush!). As for blouses, bags and shoes—a little glamour and shine is fine, but less is more professional.

ELEMENTS *of* STYLE

SECRET INGREDIENTS OF GREAT FIRST IMPRESSIONS.

DIGNIFIED WATCH
Send your neon-colored toy watches into a timeout. For business, strap on a keepsake.

1

OXFORD SHOES
In luxe materials like patent or stingray, the Ivy League staple livens up urbane pantsuits.

2

TOUT DE SWEET!
France's first lady Carla Bruni puts her signature sexy spin on the conservative suit—particularly graceful with ballerina flats.

3

BAG ORDER Don't limit yourself to an ultra-traditional top handle; choose one with gutsy details.

4

PEARL POWER Whether you get them from Grandma's jewelry box or J. Crew, pearls always look priceless.

5

Signature Style

FOR ME," says Donna Karan (pictured above), "wearing the right thing is like meditating; a way of finding calm amid the chaos." Comfort has always been primary for Karan and the key to the loyalty of her working women fan base, who spend long hours in their professional outfits. "My mentor, Anne Klein, used to say, 'A look has to have heart and soul, whether it's a gown or a hospital gown. I would definitely add 'or a business suit' to that list."

For a job interview, Karan wouldn't propose going all-out sexy, although she advocates embracing your body's sensual expression and freedom of movement. Hence, her predilection for luxurious fabrics that stretch, feel great against your skin and retain their shape—they never conspire against you in a competitive environment. "I'm flattered that some of the world's most formidable women have worn my clothes," muses Karan, "and I like to think it's because I've dressed the whole woman. I enhance her natural shape, delete the negatives—we all have them—and liberate her modern spirit."

A well-dressed working woman should exude authority but not bedazzling luxury, believes Karan. In other words your go-to office clothes should become trusted colleagues that won't outshine you. She's also a firm believer in the spiritual power of personal style—you might even say she's into lucky charms. "For years after a trip to Africa, I wore a pair of lightweight leather bracelets given to me by a Namibian woman," recalls Karan. "I literally never took them off, whether for black tie or business. They became part of me." No doubt that's what Ann Klein meant by 'soul.'

Professional must-haves (Top to bottom) Luxe-tailored suits in neutral tones; an official trench; personal tribal jewelry; a vividly colored pantsuit on Hillary Clinton; supersized gray fur collar; top handle bag in all-weather white; Body Perfect Collection Smoothing Leggings.

"Power dressing now is designed to let the woman inside us come through."

DONNA KARAN

Ladylike Top Handle

Luminous Skin

Deal Makers

Seeing yourself as more than a pretty face doesn't mean you should neglect your face—or any other part of your appearance. Think classic, natural, neat.

Neat Ponytail

Feminine Blouse

Pretty in Pink

Crazy-colored Nails

Extravagant Hairstyle

Cleopatra Eyes

Deal Breakers

As trendy and playful as these looks are for partying, when it comes to an interview, don't even think about it.

Cleavage

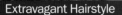

Peep-Toe Shoes

Executive Sweet

EVEN A POTENTIAL EMPLOYER at one of those hipster offices where the execs all wear jeans to work will expect you to dress up when meeting them for the first time. No need to look drab or dowdy, of course. Choosing wow colors and color variations on the suit theme will go a long way toward getting you hired.

Fresh takes on tailored
(Clockwise from top left) Ruffles refine a black pantsuit; soft knit pantsuit in caramel; neon tunic suit; big, boxy white tuxedo; traditional tweed with fierce fur trim; white jacket with artistic appliqué; yellow chiffon suit with short sleeves.

Pulling it Together

Show reverence for the job, but look ravishing, too.

W HEN GOING FOR A JOB that requires imagination and a steady stream of fresh ideas, your interview look has to multitask. It should convince the interviewer you think creatively—maybe you're bold enough for an embroidered white skirt suit or a ladylike fabric like satin that drapes for a bit of drama. But at the same time it must signal your respect for the interview process. That might mean a classic-but-better tweed suit with a bolder shoulder. Or a power red ensemble with riveting rhinestone cuffs. Last but not least, your clothes should make you feel calm, collected and ultra confident. As Isaac Mizrahi says, "The more relaxed you can get, the better you will do."

ELEMENTS *of* STYLE

A BOLD VIEW OF BUSINESS CHIC.

EXOTIC PUMP
A provocative python shoe says you can deal with danger.

1

2

27

Best Foot Forward

Pumped Up

LIKE THE BUSINESS SUIT, pumps were once worn exclusively by men and are really the go-to shoe for job interviews. Back in the 1500s, pompes were prized for their simple practicality (no buckles, laces, finery or fuss) and versatility. No wonder they evolved into the working woman's everyday shoe. Ever elegant First Lady Jacqueline Kennedy used to buy twelve pairs at a time.

INVEST IN

- ❏ Classic Oxfords in black or brown are Ivy League–smart for skirts or trouser suits.

- ❏ Dashing flat-heeled riding boots might just close the deal.

- ❏ Sheer or matte finish panty-hose that match your skin tone; opaque black for winter.

Creatively Shod

VARIATIONS ON THE PROFESSIONAL pump abound. Two-toned patent platform pumps, loafer pumps, even booties will work with well-tailored trousers. So will fantastic, luxe versions of the classic Oxford (great with pantsuits). You need to have your wits about you during an interview—not worrying about blisters, toe cleavage, or if the super-thin straps on your shoes are making your feet bleed.

Sure-Hire Handbags

BESIDES BEING an eternal object of desire, a structured top-handle bag pulls an entire look together like nothing else. And since you are purposefully underplaying your clothing, here's an occasion to really let your most functional accessory dazzle. Look for one in highly polished leather or exotic skin—real or faux.

INVEST IN

❑ An ultraluxe bag in black, brown or neutral. Worth the bucks and it might last even longer than your next job!

❑ An ostrich-, python- or crocodile-look leather.

❑ A medium-sized bag if you don't have one. This isn't the moment for a ginormous tote, knapsack or tiny clutch.

"JEWELRY ISN'T MEANT to make you look rich," decreed Coco Chanel. "It's meant to adorn you." In other words, if you want the interviewer to focus on your skills, not your sparkle, leave Granny's princess bling in the vault.

Deal-Sealing Jewelry

CHAPTER TWO

Dressing for...

Day to Night

Day to Night Looks

I'S A GIVEN that the more accomplished a woma becomes in the workplace, the more demanding he social life. Between client dinners, work-related cu tural events, letting-off-steam drinks with colleague and boyfriend time, the great working-girl challenge i finding looks that transition from day to night. Few ca spare time to nip home after work to transform them selves head-to-toe, Cinderella-like. The look you choos at 7 AM needs to work for you well past 7 PM. Naturally, day-to-night outfit shouldn't be such knockout that it screams to coworke you've got glamorous after-hours plan (Do you really want to be grilled all da about why you're so dressed up?) Kee luxe touches to a minimum: If you've opted for a broca skirt, top it with a simple cashmere cardigan; tone dow the dazzling green satin blouse with simple black pant

> ## The difference between day and night dressing is outdated."
>
> **YVES SAINT LAURENT**

PLAYLIST »

Stay fab in the fast lane with marathon pieces and transition items that work dawn 'til dusk.

■ **Luxe fabrics**
Satin, silk brocade, chiffon, leather and fur—key elements of your day-to-night transition team. **(1)**

■ **Fitted dress**
Streamlined and efficient is the message. The office isn't the place for poufs or baby-dolls—but feel free to luxe it up with a lush, vivid hue scarf. **(2)**

■ **Elegant coat or cape**
Of all the elements that build your look, the coat looms largest. **(3)**

■ **Embellished shoe**
Swap your pumps for these sparklers as you head for the door. **(4)**

■ **Cocktail ring**
Nothing says "Fun night ahead" like a jumbo whimsical cocktail ring. **(5)**

■ **Fancy bag**
Sultry, saucy, surprising . . . and smart enough to hold your evening essentials. **(6)**

All the night moves

The supremacy of menswear (sober palette and plain material) is challenged by ladylike fabrics like lurex, satin and silk (right). Solid colors suggest single-mindedness and simple chic. (Opposite, clockwise from top left) short-sleeved sheath, black jacket and mint green skirt, red and gray skirt suits in soft fluid satin.

Looks That Work and Play

A hyper-efficient AM-PM look takes care of style while you focus on work.

UNLESS YOU RELISH lugging a garment bag into work and changing in the ladies' room or traveling all the way home to get gussied up—which only cuts into happy hour—you'll see the sense of mastering style shortcuts that save you the trouble. For starters, consider the transformative power of fabrics. There's the conventional workaday double-breasted blazer in navy wool, but that's undeniably stuffy for the evening. But then there's the undeniably "wow" blazer in python-patterned moiré taffeta, which works both day and night. In the last few years, what was once strictly the stuff of evening chic: Sumptuous brocades, duchess satin, jewel-embellished silks, lace, leather and fur have all become perfectly acceptable for work.

"THE LOOK IS STILL FEMININE BUT NOT IN A ROMANTIC WAY . . . IT'S ABOUT BEING STRONG."—Miuccia Prada

A Dress Goes the Distance

AFTER DECADES of downplaying femininity in the office—suiting up in androgynous menswear and sensible but sexless shoes—women have decided that sometimes they've just got to get really dressed up. In a dress! It's fuss-free fashion that works as effectively for business as for pleasure. Simply slip on a pair of spectacular shoes and you're practically good to go. Even those designers who once staked their reputations on saucy red carpet numbers now send a parade of work-friendly options down the runway. A tailored shift, a jersey wrap dress, a full-skirted frock all project an efficient-yet-edgy image that sustain you from desk to decadent evening.

Dressing up the work dress
(Clockwise from top left) Coordinate your print dresses with print shoes; don vivid hue hose; slither into a leather jacket; get graphic in an eye-popping print; step out in power red pumps; steal the scene in a flirty pink shrug.

Straight and narrow
The ultra-simple slim sheath, indispensable for those weekday dinners, cries out for a coordinating topper.

Get the Look

Boss by day, babe by night: achieving that serious but sexy balance.

"FASHION OFFERS NO GREATER CHALLENGE than finding what works for night without looking like you're wearing a costume," says fashion mogul Vera Wang. Double ditto if you're going to work a full day in that same outfit. The perfect AM/PM look is a fashion yin yang, a balancing act between soft and sturdy, feminine and masculine. (Satin and leather perhaps? Mink and metallic? A man's watch in a pretty pastel?) How much to girl up gray flannel with gemstone embellishments depends on how conservative or funky your office is. And you gotta get the mix right. Spend time scouting out serious-but-still-sexy silhouettes that won't raise eyebrows around the watercooler. If it's pricey it may still be worth the investment: A bedazzling but costly black pantsuit may cost a few extra bucks, but if it fits you and also feels great on—pony up! Just calculate how many hours you'll spend in this outfit a year and divide by the cost . . .

ELEMENTS *of* STYLE

FIVE WAYS TO PUT PM DAZZLE IN YOUR DAYWEAR.

PRECIOUS FLAT
Talk about prima ballerinas: gemstone encrusted and jewel toned.

1

CASE FOR LACE
Neither virginal, funereal or fragile, lace embraces the workplace!

2

CUFF LOVE
Big, shiny and colorful cuffs upgrade any look.

3

TIME OUT
A classic watch in a heady merlot red. Insta-icebreaker.

4

FUR ACCENT
Rebel a little: Touch up a no-nonsense trench with a little luxe.

5

41

Sarah Easley and Beth Buccini

Signature Style

W HEN COLLEGE BESTIES Sarah Easley and Beth Buccini (pictured above) reunited after various professional stints (at Christian Dior and *New York* magazine, respectively) they pooled their talents and experience into the must-stop Manhattan shop for any fashion maven, Kirna Zabete. Keeping stock of hot labels as well as hand-picking fashion's future stars has them working around the clock. Who better to advise us on day-to-night dressing? "Keep a shopping bag full of key pieces under your desk for quick, effective changes. Trade your neutral day show for a brightly colored or wild leopard-print one. And ditch your businesslike blazer for a sequined cardigan with a metallic clutch" says Easley. Her favorite day look is a long sleeveless vest over tailored pants. Smart in the boardroom—but when cinched with a patent belt, it's genius as a cocktail frock. (Lose the pants, naturally.) Jewelry is a no-fail look-shifter. Do dangly earrings, a bold cuff or chunky cocktail ring. Just not all three together! Add a silky clutch and red lips and you've got that Kirsten Dunst as Marie Antoinette thing down!

No-fail style-shifters (Clockwise from top left) Knee-length skirt in black leather—very boss-worthy; sparkling drop earrings are drop-dead chic; embellished cardi for all temperatures; opulent cocktail ring (costume is fine!); leopard pump guarantees a wild ride; light-reflecting clutch you can't lose in the cab!

"If you're old enough to have a real job, you're too old to be wearing denim at night."

SARAH EASLEY

Dressy Shorts

Dance-friendly
Footwear

Deal Makers

From sexy stay-in-place 'dos and bitty-size
bling to heels you can work *and* dance in.

Stay-in-place Hairdo

Swell-egant Gloves

Horror Show Hair

Rock Chick Leather

In-your-face Bling

Up-to-there Skirt

Deal Breakers

Over-the-top looks can hit bottom in boardroom or bar.

Bags and Bling

Transformers

INVEST IN

❏ A chic clutch in a color bright enough to get noticed at night.

❏ A ladylike top handle in a luxe material like ostrich— why not in a playful crayon color?

❏ High-shine patent makes for a durable and distinguished day-to-nighter.

ONE MINUTE YOU'RE on a conference call at your desk, the next you're in a cab heading for the VIP room of a cool club. A bold bag can help you transition your look from one to the other. Lock up your tote at work (or leave in the limo!) and party with a sleek evening bag or clutch in a standout material.

IF THE NIGHT AHEAD demands that you shake off your workaday demeanor—and shake your booty—a little spotlight-stealing jewelry is in order. Jaw-droppingly decadent bangles, precious pendants and intoxicatingly cute cocktail rings can render the simple sheath you wore to work unrecognizably glamorous. If you've had to down-play the glam for the business lunch, bust out for evening in expressive bangles, baubles and beads.

47

Gimme Some Skin

Dare to Bare

NOTHING MORE DEPRESSING than feeling overdressed for a romantic encounter. There you are in your power pinstripes and mid-heeled pumps when suddenly you're thrust knee to knee at the local bar with the office hottie. Think fast, lass: lose the blouse, take off the tights and swap your librarian-style shoes for a pair of patent peep-toe booties. Ah, that's better. Never underestimate how priceless an accessory your own skin can be—and it's free!

INVEST IN

❑ A deep-cut, single-breasted blazer you can wear alone, sans blouse, over leggings.

❑ Peep-toe pumps—or better yet booties—or cut-out sandals. P.S. Paint your toes a trendy hue!

❑ A luxuriously sheer fabric top or dress that will seem elegant not trashy.

CHAPTER THREE

Dressing for...

a Date

The Date Look

WANT TO SEDUCE? Think reduce. A sleeveless shift, thigh-high skirt and sheer top are date-look classics: Less is always more. Skimpy doesn't have to mean girls gone wild—just a bare enough turn-on for your companion. Whatever makes you look desirous will lift your self-esteem and ensure you're genuinely yourself on the date. (Otherwise, why bother?) So, look in the mirror and ask: Does this dress accentuate my shape, boost my boobs or lengthen my legs? Ideally, yes to all of the above. Avoid at all costs a high-maintenance outfit: scratchy fabrics, too-heavy earrings, straps that fall down, stilettos that wobble, garter belts that come unsnapped. The idea is that your date—not your outfit—drive you to distraction.

A woman's dress should be like a barbed-wire fence: serving its purpose without obstructing the view."

SOPHIA LOREN

PLAYLIST »

The key to looking great on a date is keeping it simple, sexy!

■ **Soft fluid dress**
Going out in a dress you're totally mad for gets the evening off to a good start. You can't lose with a short, sleeveless number in slinky satin. (1)

■ **Something sheer**
OK, it's a bit of a tease . . . but a somewhat see-through blouse or dress will keep him guessing. (2)

■ **Embellished bag**
Sweet enough to qualify as arm candy, just big enough to stash lipstick, mirror, credit card and phone. (3)

■ **Luxe lingerie**
Unmentionables that certainly won't go without a mention après-date. (4)

■ **Whimsical jewelry**
Fun, flirty, full of celebration—think confetti made out of colorful gemstones (real or faux)—jewelry that says you're in a playful mood. (5)

■ **Girly shoe**
Invest in black or neutral strappy sandals dusted with sequins and light up the night. (6)

Sugar and spice girl
Playing coy—yes, it has a place on first dates—in a pink flower-trimmed frock (right) and romantic variations on the blush and floral theme (opposite).

Talkin' Flirty

No time like a date to indulge in a little demure "dress-up."

AREN'T CLOTHES that are "lovingly" made—sweet confections of silk chiffon layers, poetic pleats, romantic velvets and silhouettes that flow instead of squeeze and grip—exactly what you want to wear on a first date? No matter your age, you probably feel like a girl tonight so why suppress your inner Lolita? No one's suggesting school-girl-in-kneesocks (even when they're trendy). But during love's first awakening, it's not the best time for a "borrowed from the boys" look. Consign the studded biker jacket, ripped-to-shreds jeans and distressed Oxfords to the armoire and think pretty.

"I WANTED TO SHOW A LUXURY STYLE FROM THE STREET . . .

MORE PEOPLE WANT LUXURY."—Nicolas Ghesquière, Balenciaga

Passion Statements

MAYBE YOU WANT to get him back after he's strayed, or you're planning to break up and make sure he'll miss you. Could be you're going to a party with someone new, knowing your ex will be there. (Be the first to get up and dance in an emerald taffeta sheath. Your ex will turn green with envy of your new partner.) Wild night ahead? There's always a leopard sheath. Things sure to get hot? Consider red. And does anything really say "bad girl" better than black?

Well, maybe a boudoir-licious corset dress or sheer cami. Your boyfriend a-humming the Sugar Ray song "I Just Wanna Fly"? Then a feathered dress it is!

Vamping out

Simplify the elements of seduction with a sexy-as-all-get-out frock with minimal jewelry (clockwise from top left): "Hand-painted" floral chiffon mini; pleated red skater's dress with matching platform booties; lingerie-style satin skirt and matching camisole; hot pink jacket tops an LBD; sequin-splashed red dress; banded gray degrade body dress; a feathered frock in a solid color with a single bangle; short-sleeved fur jacket and embroidered mini—the quintessential rock diva look.

Venus in green
A satin mini's crisp
schoolgirl collar is
feisty at full speed.

Leading Ladies in LBDs

Think you're stressed when faced with what to wear on a date?

E VERY TIME a Hollywood A-lister makes a public appearance, her sole mission is to seduce her thousands of fans all over again. And while she has a squadron of stylists and big-name designers at her beck and call, ready to outfit her in one of the season's sweet colorful concoctions, she'll quite often opt for the pure and simple beauty of a Little Black Dress. Dramatic? That's a given, but black is also famously flattering, no matter the body type from boyish to buxom, from a perfect size 8 to pregnant. Whether posing for the paparazzi or running around town, nothing says "money shot" better than a white-hot star in black.

Women in black

Womanly is the operative word—for nothing enhances the feminine shape quite like a black dress. Marilynesque Christina Hendricks (left), and (far left to right) Jennifer Aniston in casual culottes dress; Nicole Kidman in a pouf; Sofia Coppola in a mini goddess; Brooke Shields in a stretchy flower-embellished gown that gently caresses her baby bump.

Hot Night

The look of love? Seven just-heaven variations on the theme.

T O EACH HER OWN SEDUCTION style, no? Once you're clear about your intentions for the evening—maybe you're going to flirt madly but play hard to get, or drive him into a downright frenzy of lust—dress the part. Legendary fashion editor Diana Vreeland once said, "When dressing, be absorbed completely and utterly in yourself, letting no detail escape you. However, once dressed, be interested in only those about you." Perhaps you'll appeal to his primitive mating instincts in a tribal print mini dress and jungle-elegant accessories in wild colors or titillate his interest in a skintight sheath. Some girls play coy in full-skirted '50s-style frocks, while others dazzle with hothouse pinks and tropical citrus colors. Then again, the classic satin doll in elegant stone embellishments is nothing to be toyed with.

ELEMENTS *of* STYLE

SEXY EXTRAS THAT WORK LIKE A CHARM.

CHUNKY PINK PUMP
Extra-high heel and bold white bow is tailored with a touch of the tarty.

1

TRANSPARENT TOP
A little bare, a lot of flair, sheer pieces allow for a sexy look—perfect for layering.

2

3

4

5

Signature Style

NOTHING SHORT of dazzling, Donatella Versace's party dresses are full-on fantasies for the modern good-time girl. When it comes to the art of seduction, Versace relies on, well, art: everything from neoclassical Roman florals, Greek frieze graphics, Baroque curlicues and contemporary Op Art prints. The fit flames the sexiness: super-slim body dresses, stretchy knits and flirty grabby skirts. Meticulous tailoring and the finest Italian fabric make the difference between a flimsy frock and a dress that goes the distance on a big night out.

"Creativity comes from a conflict of ideas," Donatella believes, which explains her nonchalant pairing of vivid pastel silk with slinky black leather or—as with the Roman-centurion dress Jennifer Lopez wore on an *American Idol* finale—reimagining a metal breastplate and pleated tunic in a shimmering blue chiffon print. The House of Versace was the first top label to exclusively use star power to broadcast their designs to the world, and it's not hard to imagine femme fatale fans like Madonna, Beyoncé and January Jones wearing what sways down the runway each season. But date dressing isn't simply about high-gloss finishes and flying fringe—there's a sensuality you experience only when you slip into the clothes. Versace fans appreciate the nuance: Every stunning design plays to the camera, but also has a private life all its own.

Goddess of love

Divalicious designer Donatella Versace (pictured top right) is aces at dressing for the mating game. A-list luminaries like January Jones and Madonna line up to be costumed spectacularly on stage and red carpet. (Clockwise from top left) Neon multicolored print shift; silver quilted clutch; turquoise enamel cocktail ring; red satin platform sandals; J Lo swinging the blues on *American Idol*.

" It's better to create a reaction than to create no reaction. That's dangerous. **"**

DONATELLA VERSACE

Romantic Detail

Natural Makeup

Deal Makers

Pssst! Pretty is back. Makeup kept to a minimum, lips kiss-able, and lingerie making a (sometimes) discreet appearance.

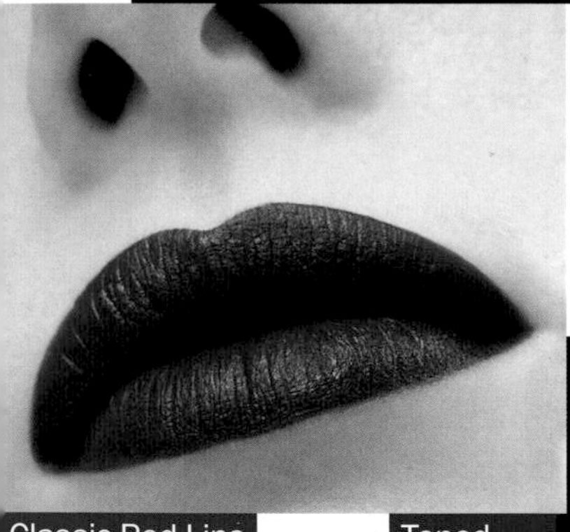

Element of Surprise

Classic Red Lips

Toned Arms and Pretty Bracelets

Three's a Crowd

Extreme Hair

Goth Black Lips

Overdoing It

THE CLASSIC ITALIAN COOK BOOK

MARCELLA HAZAN

Day-Glo Makeup

Deal Breakers

Coming on too strong's a real passion-killer. Save Goth chic (and guard dogs) for other occasions.

Armed and Fabulous

WELCOME TO THE NEW NORMAL, when we can build our entire evening look around our handbag! And why not? Clutches and embellished cross-body bags are little luxuries we actually need. After all, it's become de rigueur to stock our purses not only with basic necessities but also with items as cute as the bags themselves. Go for a classic shape in a sexy color and fabric.

INVEST IN

❏ A clutch that doubles as a conversation piece (it's that eye-catching and quirky).

❏ Purse-size makeup and fragrance that are packaged as prettily as you are.

❏ Faux gemstone jewelry that looks precious—but doesn't cause anxiety when you get up to dance!

SEXIEST FANTASIES

INVEST IN

❑ A tulle-embellished sandal ensures you're on intimate footing.

❑ An ultra-glamorous garter belt for sheer stockings—the ultimate seducer.

❑ Matching lingerie jacket set when you need just a slip of cover-up for sharing a nightcap or morning coffee.

Boudoir-Licious Lingerie

AFTER-HOUR FASHIONS now factor in the frill factor. Bras, panties, teddies and boudoir accessories are worn every which way and well out in the open at restaurants or bars—no longer saved strictly for the bedroom. Few rules apply, except to keep it sexy and slinky: As great American wit Dorothy Parker quipped: "Brevity is the soul of lingerie." Sheer genius.

CHAPTER FOUR

Dressing for...

Cool Cocktail Parties and Black Tie

The Party Look

THE INVITE SAYS "COCKTAILS" or "black tie"—so put a little party in your dress. Perhaps a punchy color, a decorated bodice, a feathered trim? Why opt for plain Mary Janes when sequined stilettos are a rave unto themselves? A thousand ways you can go, but the destination is the same: an intoxicating look. Whether short, frothy and ultra feminine; long and elegant with a twist; or something edgy and completely unexpected, your appearance should give admirers an instant mood-lift. Elle Macpherson delighted everyone when she showed up at a museum gala in a shimmering chartreuse gown and flip-flops! Compare the different re-actions to Gwyneth Paltrow's Academy Awards outfits: the rapturous applause for the cotton-candy pink taffeta ball gown she wore in 1999 and the groans all around for her sheer, black Goth getup complete with heavy kohl eyeliner in 2002. And the Oscar for Best Actress (and best dressed!) went to Paltrow thinking pink!

66 Happy, happy fashion . . .
there's not much more
to it than that. 99

MARC JACOBS

PLAYLIST »

Dress to thrill in one of these spotlight-stealers.

■ **Goddess gown**
Is it redundant to remark how divine you'll look in a floor-length goddess dress? With its ebb and flow of satin folds, your first entrance is poetry in motion. (1)

■ **Bejeweled shoe**
Finally, the expression "twinkle toes" earns some respect! Is there any doubt you'll be dancing with the stars in these? (2)

■ **Short frothy dress**
A dressy mini is like a shot of vodka; it's cool, clean and packs a punch. Talk about party favors—flirty evening frocks now come at every price point. (3)

■ **Cocktail ring**
Designed to intoxicate its admirers, a bauble with a constellation's worth of shimmer. (4)

■ **The Unexpected**
Always leave them wanting more, so the saying goes: a stunning necklace draped down the back of a plunging dress is just the ticket. (5)

■ **Luxe bag**
Think of these artsy little bags as jewelry with a job to do—holding essentials like your VIP backstage pass, perhaps. (6)

71

Dress Code Cool

Give 'em something to gossip about: sequinned jeans, chiffon skirts with biker boots and—OMG—python pouf skirts.

DRESSING DOWN A DRESSED-UP LOOK is shorthand for modern glamour. Looking too "styled," with every hair in place and button done up is, let's face it, a buzz kill. Far sexier is evening chic that embraces an easy-does-it ethos. "Take one incredibly stunning thing and put it with a pair of jeans," is how Stella McCartney sees it. Hmmm. So biker boots with a sequin frock? Or a black crisp silk gazar jacket belted over a teeny bikini . . . bottoms up!

Glam-o-rama
Putting fizz in the formal with (clockwise from top left) knockout print mini; silk gazar black jacket and bikini bottom; python pouf dress; puffy sleeve blouse with boy-cut pants; cadet-style epaulet chiffon tops; princess skirts with biker boots.

Flash forward
Sequins, the perfect party starter.

Cool Cocktails

Nothing so breathtaking as a little rule-breaking.

WHERE YOU'LL WEAR your cocktail attire affects your choice. A hip downtown art gallery, an opulent hotel drawing room, a Caribbean beach club call for an edgy, elegant or boho-glam look, respectively. Since it's a fête—let loose. Why choose a garden-variety floral for the Earth Day fundraiser when there are vivid Impressionist prints to be had? If an Afro-punk band is playing—lace up tribal sandals instead of your go-to kitten heels. (Conversation-starting shoes are a great way to break the ice.) As for the old adage, "One must suffer to be beautiful"—forget it. If drinks are served on a chilly balcony, donning a contrast-color cardi over your sheer frock proves you've got brains as well as beauty.

ELEMENTS *of* STYLE

YOUR PARTY-DRESSING CHECKLIST.

TRICKED-OUT TRENCH
Whether rhinestones, leather or fur, the military classic coat gets more decorated than a five-star general!

1

GAGA-WORTHY GLASSES
Why wait 'til New Year's or Mardi Gras? A spectacular pair of specs fast tracks you past any velvet rope.

2

FLAT AND FABULOUS
An increasing number of cool girls—from Alexa Chung to Elle Macpherson—wear fabuloso flat shoes to very fancy events.

3

VELVET FROCK
Once exclusively worn by royals, the smooth, luminous fabric known as velvet makes anyone feel like a princess.

4

OVERSIZED CUFFS
With a stack of these sassy, studded badass baubles, who needs a disco ball?

5

Red-Carpet Hits and Misses

How A-listers earn spots on the Best-and-Worst Dressed lists.

A CTRESSES INVENTED scene-stealing, so no surprise they compete for the Klieg lights just as fiercely when it comes to red-carpet clothes. Waiting for a thumbs up or thumbs down from the fashion press after an awards show wrecks nerves every bit as much as anticipating an award for your acting! Attention getting requires going pretty. And it's about the unexpected. The bold choice. Think Eva Mendes rocking a chunky turquoise choker rather than the usual diamonds with her sleek white goddess gown. The Wow factor can sometimes, surprisingly, be a simple thing. Remember quintessential California girl (and perennial best-dressed lister) Jennifer Aniston at the Oscars in 2008 accessorizing her white column with a priceless possession: a tan! Something about Jen's Venus of Venice Beach chic—all bronzed skin and tousled blond hair—sealed her fate as America's forever favorite sweetheart. In an evening of over-the-top artifice, going natural worked its magic. (There are good tans and bad. Remember the year of the bafflingly brunette Jessica Simpson with her obvious fake-bake skin and cakey makeup?)

Les freaks & les chics

Cringemaking memories (from top left to bottom left): Demi Moore in biker shorts; Whoopie Goldberg channels Little Bo Peep; a fake-baked Jessica Simpson; a Glinda-the-Good-Witch gown for Kim Basinger. Applause-worthy choices (from top right to bottom right): Eva Mendes' turquoise choker adds magic to her minimalist look; Jennifer Aniston's beachy glow matches her rhinestones; Reese Witherspoon is the diva next door in sumptuous black.

Love that red
Perennial nominee and fashion muse, Hilary Swank outranks the competition in another simply stunning gown.

Black Tie

We're so down with your gown, girl!
Designers re-fashion the formal.

IT'S ALL ABOUT THRILLING ME SOFTLY. Dressing for black-tie parties or so-called "formal" affairs these days is playing against the *Night at the Opera* image of stiff gowns and bling that only an Amazon could walk in. A lot can depend on the occasion, of course. Maybe you're going with a cute date—in which case you might choose a seductive décolleté dress. But if you're at an event representing your employer, then demure will have the desired and devastating impact. A sizzling color can add heat while a pastel will sweeten the impact of even the most classic formal frock. Let loose with saucy accessories: a tiny tiara, a flat sandal or a gemstone-studded choker go a long way toward earning you stand-out status.

ELEMENTS *of* STYLE

WHAT CITY CINDERELLAS
WEAR TO THE BALL!

URBAN TIARA
A royal rendition of the posh and oh-so-pragmatic headband.

1

CHOKER IS WILD
Now you know what they mean when they say the be-ribboned choker comes with "extra ice."

2

PEARL CRAZY
No, it's not obsessive to coordinate your precious clutch and bracelet!

3

SHEER HEAVEN
A little black dress assumes a dreamlike quality with a halo of transparent black tulle.

4

ARTY SHOES
The new shoe masterpieces take cues from painters' pastels and architects' design elements.

5

Signature Style

WHEN YOUR NAME is synonymous with dreamy ultra-chic wedding gowns—worn by style icons like Kate Hudson, Beyoncé Knowles and Victoria Beckham—the world expects not a little romance from your cocktail frocks and black-tie dresses. Between the lush Oriental silk florals, Belle Epoque corset tops, billowing satin trains and hand-ruched tulle, all in seductive shades of blush pink, poppy and marigold, Vera Wang's clothes are among the most coveted everywhere from Hollywood to Hong Kong. But that's not to say her body-loving sheaths are all sweet confection: "I was raised on Manhattan's Upper East Side but always had a downtown edge," she says. "There's a definite yin yang to my designs." New York City girl and one-time competitive ice skater, Wang creations incorporate a streetwise edge that can be dressed up or down with lacey shorts, leather bomber jackets and her trademark skater-girl leggings. Wang seems to be saying there's no one avenue to genuine chic. "After my mother took me to the Paris couture shows in the late sixties," she recalls, "I'm pretty sure I was the only high-schooler in New York going to parties in a white YSL tuxedo jacket." That same simple twist of tradition—a menswear tux as a stylish girl's cocktail classic—is the motif behind some of her celebrated red-carpet winners: the glamorous sequined T-shirt gown Joan Allen wore to the Oscars, or the plunging bright yellow Victorian-style gown Michelle Williams wore to the Oscars—accessorized with little more than fire engine–red lipstick! Like many fashion moguls, Wang is detail-oriented and never misses an opportunity to subvert traditional elegance with a bold accent—say a pink gauzy mini with a black biker boot or sporty leggings with slinky python sandals.

Wang's otherworld Native New Yorker Wang (pictured top right) and her unique urban ethereality (from top to bottom): pink tulle cocktail frock with biker boots, mesh and pearl necklace, red Chinese peplum tunic, pink satin sandal, Michelle Williams in Victorian-inspired Vera at the Oscars.

" I go to the past for research. I need to know what came before so I can break the rules."

VERA WANG

Loose, Wavy Goddess Hair

Runway-ravishing
Makeup Palette

Sparkling Eyes and Cheeks

Messy Hair and Rhinestones

Deal Makers

Who's the fairest of them all? Think feminine, fresh-scrubbed and kissable with just a dusting of sparkle.

Thigh-revealing Stockings

Obvious Cosmetic Surgery

Costume-caliber Makeup

Deal Breakers

Are you wearing the look—or the look you? Minimize makeup, fragrance, hairdo and handbag!

'70s Rocker Frizz

Ginormous Clutch

Wood-nymph-worthy 'Do

Cocktail Rings for Every Cocktail

INVEST IN

❏ Sensational colored stones, either precious or semi. You'll lust after their lustre forever.

❏ Ginormous geometrics in metal or chunky crystal are like architecture at your fingertips.

❏ Think punk with fierce symbols like serpents, spikes, skulls. Great protection, too!

AS LONG AS YOU'RE SWANNING around glass in hand, might as well be flashing some serious bling. The oversized cocktail ring debuted as an evening style statement in the '50s (when nice girls did drink!). Never to be confused with a chaste wedding band, it's worn quite dramatically on the index or middle finger of your right hand. Provocative symbols, wild animal motifs and supersized stones add instant wit and glitter to any glam wardrobe.

Luxe Bags and Shoes: A Love Match

THE PERFECT ESCORT is someone who complements but doesn't mirror you. The same goes for party shoes and bags. No matter how hyper-vivid the colors or whimsical the embellishments, they should coordinate, not compete. (Bonus points for also tying in your makeup palette!) A platform stiletto sandal in nude and black jives nicely with either a neutral or black python clutch. Tickle someone's fancy with black feathered bags and heels.

INVEST IN

❏ Boudoir-luxe accents like feathers, pom poms and anything nude.

❏ A mine-full of silver cuffs, clutches, metallic makeup (used minimally).

❏ Exotic skin evening bags, slinky stilettos or flats. Eternally ssssexy.

CHAPTER FIVE

Dressing for...

Clubs and Concerts

Dressed to Groove

WHAT DOES IT TAKE to get an otherwise demure female to slither into studded leather and stilettos, ravaged jeans and rhinestones or killer cowboy boots and bustiers? When she's out raving to her fave tunes at a club or concert, duh. Rewind to the '80s with MTV videos of Madonna playing 24/7 while Material Girl styles proliferated at the mall. No wonder an entire generation became instantly defined by its maverick music icon. Since then pop star chic has reached a crescendo: Think of the fashion influence of Gwen Stefani, Rihanna, Missy Elliott, Jessica Simpson and Lady Gaga. Some not only influence designers, they are designers. Anyone gonna debate the insta-impact on American tweens of "Whip My Hair" songbird Willow Smith, whose onstage getups include leather vests, leopard harem pants and press-on nails with silver teddy bear charms? Girls just wanna have fun letting loose their inner divas.

"Our beauty standard has become harder and tougher because we live in a tough age."

PLAYLIST»

Rock a look that says I'm with the band.

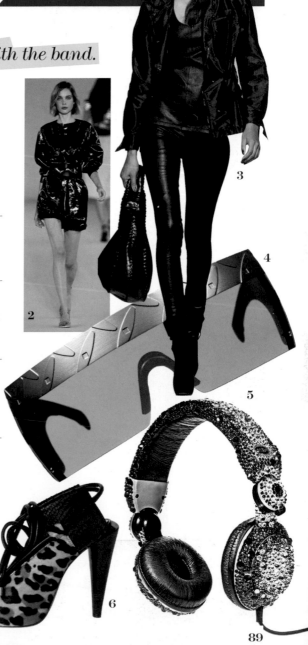

1

■ Chain jewelry

Wearing shiny metal chains has been a favorite attention-getting scheme of everyone from Egyptian queens and Renaissance kings to hip-hop moguls and sophisticated Chanel devotees. From rosary bead delicate to biker chain bulky. **(1)**

■ Metallic fabric

No need to be into heavy metal to appreciate the glitter and glam effects of lurex. **(2)**

■ Leather jacket or pants

Redefine second skin with airtight leather pants that make you look like you just pulled up to the club on your Harley. **(3)**

■ Shades

No bouncer's going to keep you waiting behind the velvet rope for long if you're sporting a pair of fierce shades. Paparazzi bait? You bet. **(4)**

■ Haute headphones

Quintessential electronic chic—crystal-studded earphones—to wear to, from and possibly during your evening out (if the music's too loud!). Think of it as bling—so tone down the necklaces and other baubles. **(5)**

■ Dancing shoes

Leopard stilettos, leather booties, kick-ass cowboys and updated Beatle boots—perfect footwear for every playlist. **(6)**

2

3

4

5

6

Rock Star Chic

Burn up the dance floor in sizzling, slinky looks.

YOU HEAR A LOT about "the mix" in music—combining elements to get the sound you want—well, ditto rock star style. It's about stealing the spotlight with edgy elegance, luxed-up street style, fierce femininity. Yo, Katy Perry in a faux leopard coat and bare legs and Alexandra Richards (daughter of Rolling Stones' Keith) in retro schoolboy blazer.

Style follows soundtrack
Choose from (clockwise from top left) disco ball glitter; heavy metal leather; Mod '60s animal prints; grunge camo; Katy Perry in leopard; rock royalty Alexandra Richards transforms a traditional blazer; a fur vest boldly worn as a bustier.

Mix master
Bustle and flow in long chiffon skirt and pearls, then cut the sweetness with studded leather jacket and killer platform bikers.

Rock it!

Rock star style riffs off iconic pieces of rebellious youth: T's, jeans, leather.

THE FIRST PRINCESS OF PUNK Debbie Harry once proclaimed, "I feel one of the things I brought to rock 'n' roll was that sort of movie-star glamour." Certainly her signature look, a brilliant clash of her kitschy T's and ripped jeans with screen siren red lips and teased peroxide hair was career-making. Iconoclastic, rebellious—just like her music—her look was ultimately attainable. Rock chic isn't about couture, it's about cool. It's daring, fresh and forever young. When Courtney Love famously wore a tiara, it was like a little girl playing princess; the Pretenders' Chryssie Hynde still rocks out—as chicly androgynous as ever in her late 50s—in tight little boy T-shirts and skinny pants.

ELEMENTS *of* STYLE

SAMPLE THESE LOOKS FROM GLAM ROCK, GRUNGE OR HEAVY METAL.

ELECTRIC PUMPS
Funky fur-trimmed blue suede shoes? You can do anything but stay off them!

1

BLING FATALE
Fancy a touch of tough with your romantic floral print? Add a pair of silver and gold thorn bracelets.

2

ELVIS JACKET
The King's signature gold jacket refashioned for girls—no finer partner for black leggings and bouffant 'do.

3

BIKER BOOTS
The iconic cool girl boot—a supermodel's staple—is ready to rumble at gritty biker bars and chic city brasseries alike.

4

RETRO SHADES
No shortage of nerd-chic frames immortalized by legendary rock stars—from Buddy Holly to John Lennon. Here, the Black Wayfarers favored by Michael Jackson.

5

A Twang thang
Hick meets haute:
(Right) Rancho
deluxe white pet-
ticoat; (Opposite,
from left) turquoise
bling emboldens
black; patchwork
shift; Daisy Duke-ish
bustiers.

Country Strong

For hippie chicks and Nashville vixens, it's romance with a shot of rugged.

FRAYED blue jeans, cowboy boots, fringed suede and hippie prints have become such staples in modern wardrobes even among city dwellers, it's easy to overlook their country roots. Blonde ringleted Taylor Swift—sort of a Nashville Venus—might occasionally swap her floral-print sweetheart frocks for Dior chiffon gowns, but her cowboy boots usually stay put. Gretchen "Redneck Woman" Wilson adds a crocheted bikini top to her signature cutoffs with a big studded silver belt—so why can't you? When The Indigo Girls and their myriad fans don their classic Western shirts (complete with embellished yoke and pearl snap buttons), the look is gutsy, natural, honest—just like their folk rock tunes.

"LUXURY MUST BE COMFORTABLE, OTHERWISE IT'S NOT LUXURY."—COCO CHANEL

Country Western Chic

Boost your country cred with cowgirl fringe, denim and Navajo bling.

NSPIRING, SURPRISING, SEXY in an innocent way, country western chic is where traditional all-American silhouettes meet gutsy glamour. No wonder there's an increasing down-home vibe on both runway and red carpet, with the likes of Carrie Underwood, Miley Cyrus and Taylor Swift right at the top of Best-Dressed Lists with the best of them. Millicent Rogers, early-20th-century heiress and godmother of "rancho deluxe" dressing, used to adorn her Paris-purchased Balenciaga gowns with piles of chunky turquoise and engraved silver. Well, she's as much of a muse to today's top designers as citified icons like Audrey Hepburn.

ELEMENTS *of* STYLE

HOW THE WEST WAS WORN.
HERE ARE FIVE WAYS. »

FRINGE BOOTS
Ranch dressing for the feet: suede fringe boots for any ol' hoedown.

1

COWGIRL BLUES
Stand by your denim, whether cutoffs, scarves or cross-body bags.

2

BANDANNA PRINTS
You can bet the ranch, designers will mine the West for their best ideas.

3

NATIVE BLING
Trade in your diamonds for turquoise to get the ultimate in sheriff chic.

4

SWEET DRESSES
Even rugged country gals will fall for flouncy little floral frocks.

5

Leave it to Divas

WHILE LEGENDARY CROONER Frank Sinatra had millions of male fans reaching for fedoras, his daughter Nancy gets credit as the first female pop style icon—and even had a hit song to go with it. "These Boots Are Made for Walkin'," which broke in 1966, also immortalized her white go-go boots—still iconic today. No need to dress head-to-toe diva; it's enough to cherry pick—perhaps a Madonna-style bustier or Beyoncé's hoodie—to hit your own high style note.

Good time glam (Clockwise from left) Madonna growls in a catsuit; Rihanna glows in neon 'do; Gaga the glamorous; Christina Aguilera vamps it up in a leopard onesie; Taylor Swift's floral Prints Charming!

Urban renewal
Who better than
Beyoncé to haute-up a
hoodie and put a chic
spin on biker chains?

Signature Style

WITH A REBEL YELL, fans of Alexander McQueen clothes cry for more punk-tinged jewelry, shocking fabrics and outrageous platforms. The same legendary London-based label that dressed Kate Middleton in the pure white perfection of a wedding gown also swings to the opposite extreme as the go-to label for radical, raucous rock chicks and the fans who dress like them. Since the founding designer's untimely death in 2010, the beat goes on under Creative Director Sarah Burton (pictured above) and her iconoclastic interpretation of romance. Like the stars who favor the label—Gaga, Rihanna, Beyoncé—McQueen designs weave together feminine fragility and strength, exuding glamour with a savage streak. "Clothes and jewelry should be startling, individual," McQueen once said. "When you see a woman in my clothes, you want to know more about her." Certainly Beyoncé mixing up a McQueen velvet military jacket with liquid-looking leggings and gladiator sandals is a look all her own: self-confident and fearless, yet with a distinct nod to strict traditional tailoring. From shredded leather pantsuits and Baroque gold wedges to a black lace Goth-meets-prim-Victorian party dress, there's plenty of paradox to play around with to achieve a scene-stealing club look. Think costume-like but wearable, frivolous but thought-provoking, vulnerable yet with a hard, protective edge. McQueen girls are rock royalty who parade in alluring armor.

Rock treatment
Scene-stealing McQueens (from top to bottom) Heidi Klum in Behemoth platforms; Beyoncé performs in military velvet; cut-out buckle booties, Goth Girl prom dress; gold skull bangles.

Shred heads
Burton dances
divas over to
the dark side in
cute-meets-kinky
lasercut leather
pantsuits.

Groovy 'Do

Punk-rock Tights

Deal Makers

Sweat-proof
Matte Lips

Smudged eyes, red matte lips, artfully
messed hair. To paraphrase T-Pain: You hit
the club and you're ready for the dance floor!

Smudged Eyes

Rock-royal Purples

Gone
Platinum

Deal Breakers

Leave glitzy, disco-ball dazzling Day-Glo to the performers. Otherwise, you'll scare off your date.

Geisha-gone-wild Hair

Ten Ton Earrings

Unearthly Eye Shadows

Ankle-breaking Pumps

Chained Melody

TALK ABOUT hyperlinks. From multiple strands of shiny gold chains with fine, lightweight links; heavy solid biker chains hanging tough as necklaces, bracelets and earrings; to metallic embellishments for belts, corsets and even boots—the classic jewelry motif has been enthusiastically adopted both by classic Chanelesque ladies and rebellious biker babes. Wearing gold chains dates to the ancient Egyptians who liked to wear several fine ropes studded with lapis lazuli. Later, the Romans added stones and eventually, spiritual talismans. Charming!

INVEST IN

❑ Biker-style gold link necklaces (real or costume).

❑ Ladylike brooches with pearls and fabrics.

❑ Metal-embellished corsets or T-shirts.

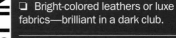

❏ Bright-colored leathers or luxe fabrics—brilliant in a dark club.

❏ Glam-rock studs that groove to the music.

❏ A size and shape you can wear while dancing, but also stash your essentials.

Bopping Bags

BORROWED FROM MESSENGERS who wear them riding bikes or scooters, extra long-strapped bags are ideal for dancing. Cross-body bags can be brightly colored and glam-rock studded in an array of dressy fabrics, but are far superior to clutches because, naturally, you can boogie with your hands free! Ideal sizes are just big enough to hold your credit card, phone, lipstick, compact and keys.

CHAPTER SIX

Dressing for…

Official Functions

Special-Occasion Dressing

ONCE YOU'VE OUTGROWN your flower girl days, it's to your benefit to know exactly which occasions call for grown-up chic. Cutesy or sex kitten just doesn't cut it when your presence is requested in a church or synagogue, or required in a courtroom. This should go without saying—but, well, we've all seen paparazzi pictures of pop tarts leaving even the grandest Federal-style courthouse in stilettos and leather minis. In fact, taking your style cues from your surroundings is never a bad idea. A wedding in an opulent marble and gold Baroque chapel calls for an elegant silk frock, not a casual cotton sundress. Rebelling against "decorum" in these instances could cause you to lose friends—or perhaps your court case.

"In matters of grave importance, style, not sincerity, is the vital thing."

OSCAR WILDE, IRISH WRITER AND MAN OF DISCERNING TASTE

PLAYLIST»

Dress to impress in one of these oh-so-subtle scene stealers.

■ **Little bit o' luxe**

Refined retro-style headbands in velvet or mink echo a bold fur shoulder piece—two bold black accents that call attention to your face. (1)

■ **Coquette dress**

Its demure below-knee length and short sleeves attest to its good taste, while the filmy florals betray the wearer's inner flirt. (2)

■ **Statement black coat**

What does a style maven reach for when the occasion calls for black? A shape-enhancing coat in a sinfully rich texture like fur (real or faux)—worn with bare legs! (3)

■ **Blush-colored handbag**

Nix the neons for serious outings. Instead look for a natural selection of neutral tones like pink, sandy and bone. (4)

■ **Understated sexy shoe**

If a shoe with killer heels is the one thing you can never forsake—even for funerals—choose a simple pair in the most low-key colors you can find. (5)

■ **Pearls rule**

Accessorize like you mean it. Special occasions call for appropriate jewelry—strings of pearls, for instance, not supersized spiked chokers. (6)

Call the toppers
Expressive details like a shawl neck (right) and fuchsia fur sleeves (opposite, center); zip pockets and velvet trim (opposite, left and right) create drama sans costume.

Get Out
the Coat

*It's all about hue,
re-charged classic cuts
and bedazzling details.*

THERE'S A REASON they're called "statement coats." Whether processing into a house of worship for a memorial or an outdoor stadium for your beau's law school graduation, all eyes will be on you. (Your own private red-carpet moment.) In fact, your arriving or departing in style in a spectacular topper with ingeniously co-ordinated bag and shoes may be the visual memory you leave people with. A manteau for all seasons? Indeed. Goes without saying you'll need that coat for blustery weather; but even when it's blistering hot outside, the AC may be cranked up to arctic levels indoors and you'll be glad you had a brilliant Spring wrap on hand. Special-occasion coats should guarantee some fun in the functional: Recharge a classic cut with a high-voltage hue, or embellish an everyday coat with a dusting of sequins, a fur trim or bedazzling belt.

"A MAN WITH A GOOD COAT UPON HIS BACK MEETS WITH A BETTER RECEPTION

THAN HE WHO HAS A BAD ONE."—Samuel Johnson, 18th-century English essayist and critic

111

Grand Entrances

Don't shy away from attention-getting coats in opulent or luxe-trimmed fabric.

P RECISELY BECAUSE a great coat is an attention-getting entrance-maker is all the more reason why, for special occasions, you want a cool classic—not a gone-tomorrow trend. Aim for a versatile, universally flattering silhouette—one that's narrow, figure-skimming and falls somewhere around the knee. Generally the taller you are, the longer the length can be; more petite types do better with knee-lengths. You can always take a simple shape to the max with texture: Subtle brocades, smooth leather details and a variety of furs—real and faux—will allow a coat to slip seamlessly from a day to evening event. Drum up a little more drama with a sprinkling of shiny gold buttons, a detachable cape, velvet cuffs, exotic print linings or lace embellishments.

ELEMENTS *of* STYLE

COAT'S THE HEADLINER? MEET SOME BRILLIANT BACKUP.

EXOTIC BAG
The shape is traditional, the material luxe, the color arresting!

1

DEMURE HEADBAND
When the occasion definitely doesn't call for bed head or beach waves.

2

BLACK SHADES
Don't let the crowd or cameras know what your eyes are saying.

3

GOLD CHAINS
Just like in the days of Henry VIII, luxury lovers wear their most precious necklaces on the outside of their coats.

4

TIMELESS HAT
Special occasions call for a nod to tradition; do it in style with a formal chapeau.

5

Standing on Ceremony

Speak the language of formal dress tradition but with your own modern accent.

D ESPITE THE INCREASING ACCEPTANCE of casual dress for social occasions, there are certain affairs for which dressing with dignity is not just a conventional social gesture but an act of courtesy—the sartorial equivalent of shaking hands and saying please and thank you. Even celebrity style icons whose signature look is outlandish take the high road for rites of passages like presidential inaugurations, awards ceremonies, brisses, baptisms and funerals.

Mourning becomes her (From top left to bottom) Kate Moss, Naomi Campbell and Daphne Guinness (in surreal platforms) at Alexander McQueen's funeral in 2010.

Wedding guests gone glam (From top center to bottom right) Jil Sander's T-shirts cum gowns; Victoria Beckham in her own all-navy design; Royal maid of honor Pippa Middleton looking priceless in emerald; a red graphic print adds a tropical punch.

She's so refined
Living proof that sophisticated ladies are stylish down to their fingertips. Same color gloves elongate the arm for a sleek, elegant look.

Fashion Judgment Day

Which stars in court are most guilty of
crimes of fashion?

Even before the judge weighed in, the fashion police (a.k.a. the tabloids) found Lindsay Lohan guilty of violating the rules of decorum when she showed up for court in a see-through, skin-tight top and six-inch platforms. (Incidently, that time Lilo got jail, not bail. Coincidence?) Besides overtly sexy styles, common fashion infractions for official business include casual jeans, wrinkled, rumpled clothes and cat-eye makeup better suited to a club crawl. Never fear: Looking respectable in an elegant suit and a sophisticated 'do can be quite arresting!

Age of innocence?
(Top, left and center) Accused A-listers dressed like good girls (following their lawyers' advice): Winona Ryder and Naomi Campbell. Those who played to the paparazzi (top right and bottom): Lindsay Lohan, and Foxy Brown.

Laws of gravity
A lanky, loose-fit houndstooth suit sends a calm, un-ruffled message.

Signature Style

T HERE'S NOTHING LIKE a royal wedding to get people talking about pageantry and protocol and what people wear for super-special occasions," says Tim Gunn (pictured above). "While Prince Will and Kate's Big Day was in England—Mecca for Mad Hatters—it was hard to miss how many aristos and A-listers played second fiddle to their own chapeau. I have great respect for fabulousness but not when an accessory assumes the role of an avant-garde sculpture atop one's shoulders! I'd have to single out royal cousin Lady Frederick Windsor as getting it right top to toe: Her perfectly fitting navy suit offset a dark blue Philip Treacy hat, which added whimsy without getting the world's tongues wagging. I predict a huge surge in the popularity of hats for formal events, thanks to Kate Middleton; they'll be worn with hair down, as she does, to give it a modern twist (see page 122).

Good and proper
Making it official (from top to bottom): white trench, knee-length black dress; Lady Windsor's royally perfect chapeau; Anna Dello Russo in long-hair-with-formal hat; duffle deluxe.

"As for dresses, for most formal occasions the best route is A-line skirt, three-quarter sleeves and a V-neck. For weddings, choose a flattering saturated color, the kind you'd find in a garden—weddings are a celebration of life, after all. But, everyone needs at least one black dress. Period. Two inches above or right below the knee—longer than that looks dowdy. By the way, V-neck doesn't mean you can sport extreme cleavage; provocative clothing that may offend certain people crosses a boundary. As for your arrival look—I sing the praises of the trench. It doesn't have to be the classic khaki gabardine. You can indulge in a shiny embellishments, a creative print or sassy color. All in all, this military-style staple will ensure you're commanding respect from the get-go.

"Before you decide on a look, ask a trusted friend how you look. You may have paid dearly for something—a dress, a pair of shoes, a hat—and feel determined to wear it even if it doesn't honestly suit you. But keep in mind: What doesn't stink to you might stink to everyone else."

"The clothes we wear send a clear message, and we're responsible for every nuance."

TIM GUNN

Understated Manicure

Power Lips Matched to Outfit

Downplay the Updo

Jewel-toned Satin Frocks

Timeless Cameo and Prim White Collar

Deal Makers

What's in your etiquette kit? Treasure hunt for vintage
jewelry like cameos; match your lips to a classic red coat.

Deal Breakers

Try to remember why you're here! If you're a wedding guest, not the bride—don't dress to distract. Called into court? Don't provoke the jury with sexed-up styles.

Bangs Overdue for a Trim

Inappropriately Casual

Racy Rhinestone Heels

Phantasmagoric Fur Hat

Maximum Exposure

Top This!

THEY'VE BEEN called "jewelry for the head" and there's no denying decorative hats have become increasingly luxe and fanciful. Any doubt that Prince William's marriage to big-brim favoring beauty Kate Middleton will launch a global clamoring for these glamorous accessories?

INVEST IN

❑ Classic wide brims, the most sun protection possible.

❑ Ladylike embellishments like tulle and silk flowers.

❑ Classic menswear shapes like cadet caps, fedoras and top hats.

Glove Affair

THE RETURN TO LADYLIKE coincides with society's hand-sanitizer obsession—so elegant gloves at a formal affair are a win-win. From perforated powder-pink suede and sexy mesh fingerless versions to classic Jackie O–style black and white, short or opera length, there's no end of elegant options.

INVEST IN

❏ White gloves: When the moment calls for Grace Kelly glam.

❏ Fashion-forward fingerless styles for flaunting oversized cocktail rings.

❏ Opera-length gloves ensure you're diva-licious whatever the occasion.

CHAPTER SEVEN

Dressing for…

a City Weekend

Urban Playdate

S O, HOW DO YOU TWEAK those chic urban looks you love on the catwalk to make them work on the sidewalk? Strolling around a city on weekends—whether seeing museums or trolling flea markets—begs the question: Can you look cool without flaunting your assets—in all senses of the word? How high is too high a heel? (Depends how much you've budgeted for taxis.) How short your skirt should be may depend if you've got a coat in case you want a cover-up. And, finally, can you wear your new diamond hoops? (If you keep them small and discreet so as not to attract the wrong kind of attention.) Thanks to the casualization of high fashion, there's no shortage of fun, viable options: killer biker boots and ultra-feminine flats that can endure hours of walking; chic but durable toppers that anticipate an unforeseen change in the weather; and luxe but lightweight totes your fatigued arms will be grateful for by the time you park your bottom on a barstool for happy hour.

"It's so modern to wear something that's easy, that travels well."

CALVIN KLEIN

PLAYLIST »

A lust-list for looking cool and pretty in places both glam and gritty.

■ **Leopard**
Big cat chic rules the urban jungle, adding a savage touch to everything from military to preppy. **(1)**

■ **Trench**
The military classic for stylish maneuvering in any metropolis. Seek out sexy fabric variations on the canvas original. **(2)**

■ **Leather/jeans remix**
Every rocker's favorite combo: a little bit biker plus a little bit cowboy ensures your look's got rhythm and blues (i.e. denim!) **(3)**

■ **Riding boots**
Glamour and ease at full gallop. Shiny, flat leather boots that upgrade everything from leggings to short shorts. **(4)**

■ **Carryall**
Always a case of size and form following function: Toting tons? Think titanic-size. **(5)**

■ **Armor-like bling**
Chunky bangles and fierce amulets that swing from chains render you street-ready. **(6)**

1

2

3

4

5

6

Chic entrenched
Nothing says "creative casual" as eloquently as a denim dress and arty-printed coat.

Uptown Express

Flirting with modern menswear puts the "city" in simplicity.

T HE TRICK to weekend dressing for the smart part of town: Feeling comfortable but confident enough not to freak if you run into Blake Lively. Kidding, but let's not pretend other pedestrians—of both sexes—aren't going to check out what you're wearing. Cool cafés, modern art galleries and designer boutiques are all places to see and be seen. Why do you think there are so many paparazzi out snapping street fashion on big city street corners? So inject some urbane into your urban look. Toughen up pretty prints with a man-tailored shirt or military trench. Show off sophisticated black with a cool contrast color.

"YOU HAVE TO ASK YOURSELF, 'HOW MANY WAYS COULD I WEAR THIS? COULD I WEAR IT TO WORK? TO DINNER OR DRINKS? WILL IT SPAN THE SEASONS?'"—Michael Kors

How Street It Is

*Park prim and preppy looks in the 'burbs.
Rev up your edgy faves for the city.*

VROOMING AROUND on a Vespa—if only virtually? Then kick-start your decadent downtown look with a little black leather. There's no better style accelerant. From there you can swing between biker, nerd chic (retro-framed glasses), intellectual boho (tie-dyed jeans), and edgy prepster (denim puffer vest). The epicenter of cool? Wherever you are, city chick.

Motorcycle style diaries
(Clockwise from top left) Denim puffer vest; cropped boyfriend blazer; bleached out gray skinnies; tie-dyed capris with punk T-shirt; black lizard vest; tight-fit metallic bomber; shredded micro jean shorts.

Leather underground
Anyone can do tight-legged leather. Instead, knock 'em dead with an unexpectedly racy, roomy pair.

Divas in Distressed

Off-camera, different denim strokes for different famous folks.

Ladies in blue
Model Erin Wasson earns street cred in shreds (left), Katie Holmes on a roll in baggies (center); Rihanna tops white wide-legs with a badass jean jacket (right).

Great jean pool
A-listers covet their downtime—and three guesses what they wear? Mandy Moore typifies the trend toward tough with an innocent twist.

Get the Look

Two different routes to Gotham pretty: uptown elegant and downtown decadent.

LADY OR VAMP? Gossip girl or rock star? There's a bit of each in all of us, so why not dress according to mood—and destination? Ivy League luxe, beloved by uptowners, draws on WASP classics like slouchy-fit shirt-collared dresses and flat sandals in sinfully rich fabrics like silk and suede. Meanwhile, "God Bless Saturday" as Kid Rock sings, for that's when downtown divas come out to play in retro toppers, sexy shorts and Oxford shoes. In fact, shorts—even in winter with tights and boots—will steal the show.

ELEMENTS *of* STYLE

CITY ESSENTIALS: GET 'EM WHILE THEY'RE HOT.

UPTOWN/ DOWNTOWN JACKET
A black leather biker walks on the mild side when mixed with posh pastel tweed.

1

SAVAGE IPAD SLEEVES
Your number one new fave accessory is probably something electronic: Protect it in style.

2

ABSTRACT SKINNY JEANS
What better look for downtown gallery hopping? Top with a white T.

3

HIGH-STYLE HIGH TOPS
The classic canvas sneaker sends designer imaginations soaring.

4

COOL-GIRL SHADES
Nerdy cool eyewear frames the windows to your soul.

5

135

Christopher Bailey

Signature Style

F ASHION FORECAST: The buzzword for sexy in the city will be Burberry for many years to come. The way chief designer Christopher Bailey ingeniously juxtaposes leather biker jackets and chiffon frocks, iconic trenches and goddess draping, military neutrals with super-saturated colors all adds up to the kind of modern armor smart girls opt for when out on the town. "Movies, rock music, people on the street—it all comes into play when I'm designing," says Bailey. "I take a lot of inspiration from the disheveled elegance of the English." It's no doubt that tug-o-war between the brand's tradition—founded by British Army outfitter Thomas Burberry in 1856—and Bailey's own cool London spin generates so much heat each season. Typically English—though it's redefining urban dressing everywhere from New York to Paris to Tokyo—is the wit and irreverence; a cropped, quilted trench cinched by a neon-green python belt, a jungle jumble of leopard and cobra prints or a leather sleeve so studded with spikes it would give a genuine English punk pause. What gives the Burberry repertoire edge is its day-to-night adaptability: the slick protective outerwear, often with metal or rubber hardware that pairs so effortlessly with leggings, mini skirts or the new floor-length. Gives new significance to the term "street-wise."

Join the stud club
Christopher Bailey (top right, shown at left, with model) is the go-to guy for on-trend trenches— just ask Emma Watson (top left) and Kate Middleton. Lately he's added studded biker leathers and animal-print silks clashed together (opposite). Utilitarian bags and six-inch boots complete the urban chic kit.

"The British have an aristocratic, noble history, but it is always contrasted with something rebellious."

CHRISTOPHER BAILEY

Not Much Ado 'Do

Incognito Shades

Deal Makers

Pay more than lip service to low-maintenance makeup, hair and skirt lengths.

Longer Skirts

Step Lively Flat

Barely There Makeup

Unabashed Bling

Labor-intensive Lips

Deal Breakers

After a day in town, these looks won't hold up for anything.

Midriff Raff

Treacherous Stilettos

Say Nay to Spray

Reboot Your Look

SCOUR THE STREETS of any modern metropolis and you'll find killer boots that walk the line between posh and protective. In addition to cool weather classics like leather thigh-highs and utilitarian rubber-soled shearlings, there are now summerized versions in canvas and cloth with perforated fabrics and peep toes.

INVEST IN

❑ Over-the-knee styles that double as leg warmers.

❑ Embellished biker or cowboy boots that take a walk on the wild side.

❑ Traditional riding boots in an unexpectedly girly hue.

Cool Carryalls

KEEP IT SIMPLE, STYLISTA. Walk tall and carry a big bag for days in the big city. Not only should it look va-va-voom, it should zip or snap closed to secure your city survival kit: wallet, phone, keys, iPod, as well as an extra pair of flats if you insist on wearing heels part of the day.

INVEST IN

❑ An easy-to-carry chain bag that works with everything from Day-Glo hues to pared-down palettes.

❑ A messenger-inspired satchel that can be switched from shoulder to shoulder.

❑ A drawstring bag or knapsack in a refined material like fur or quilted leather.

CHAPTER EIGHT

Dressing for...

a Country Weekend

> ## [Think] sport utility done in a dressed-up way."
>
> RALPH LAUREN

Country Weekend Wear

NATURE CALLS! Weekends spent mostly outdoors present a sizeable challenge: how to outfit yourself to brave the elements—extreme heat or bone-chilling cold and everything in between—without sacrificing chic. Personal downtime is when practical, easy shapes and fabrics reclaim a position of power, but don't be afraid to exhibit a little pioneer spirit. Stake your style claim by loading up a laid-back beachcomber look and ripped jeans with colorful bling or romancing a rugged pair of fringe suede pants with a silver lamé shirt. Maybe gild a crisp, sand-toned safari look with a metallic leather bomber. Designers are clearly having a field day with traditional utilitarian elements—biker boots in vivid hues, color-blocked messenger bags in luxe leathers. The sky's the limit when hardworking materials and casual classics let loose

PLAYLIST »

Weed out flimsy trends in favor of outdoorsy classics with a twist.

■ ## Safari chic

Out of Africa is never out of style, as designers offer fresh variations—khaki shorts, metallics—on the timeless huntress look. **(1)**

■ ## Trapper hat

Get a head start on keeping out the cold—invest in a fabulous fur trapper hat, found in natural and neon colors. **(2)**

■ ## Puffer vest

See the '80s preppy fave—the puffer vest—enjoy new versatility in unexpected patterns like checks, florals and camo. **(3)**

■ ## Hiker/biker boot

Ain't no mountain high enough—or city street tough enough—to diminish the impact of a sexy tough-girl boot. **(4)**

■ ## Creative cape

A brightly patterned cape is a timeless rustic staple—and it's one size fits all! **(5)**

■ ## Supersized satchel

The ideal bag for weekend suits your country casual look—but stands out just enough (say with a bright color or oversized clasp) to keep things interesting. **(6)**

1

2

3

4

5

6

Cold Play

Designers enjoy a real workout refashioning athletic gear into winning looks.

"

WHEN IT COMES TO cool casual, it's crucial to speak fashion and sport equally fluently," says Olympic skier-cum-legendary skiwear designer Willy Bogner. "That's the American spirit." Indeed, the great majority of winter wear makes no attempt to hide its origins in active sports with witty takes on everything from ski pants, snowboard jackets, hiking boots, track suits, skating skirts and even jodhpurs.

Rough and ready
(Clockwise from top left) Aviator jacket with mini skirt; olive knit sweats worn with fur; red striped track pants, green python stadium coat; quilted coat with ski pants; trekker boots and bikini bottom; checked equestrian jacket.

Rodeo drive
The sheer luxury of shearling against bare skin: a seductive pardner to cowgirl jeans.

Unbeatably chic
When deconstructed combat boots ground a pleated mini and polished leather vest, military style earns a medal for at-ease chic.

Sunny
Side Up

*Catch her if you can!
The first to merge
runway trends and
racy, athletic chic wins.*

WINNING LOOKS take on new meaning in warm weather. Even the most blatant sportswear references like sailor stripes, swim-inspired tanks and pleated tennis skirts are worn with playfully imaginative embellishments and accessories. But spring and summer weekend wear is also about showcasing skin! Bare legs and arms, midriffs and toes are meant to bask in the light of day, feel the breeze and get tickled by sand or surf. Color palettes are generally nature-inspired, whether sun-bleached sand and stone, the vivid hues of tropical plants or the preppy primaries of nautical blues and sunny brights.

"I'VE ALWAYS THOUGHT OF THE T-SHIRT AS

THE ALPHA AND OMEGA OF THE FASHION ALPHABET."—Giorgio Armani

Jock Tactics

AFTER WINNING HIS UMPTEENTH GOLD medal, snowboard Olympian Shaun White noticed his Twitter fans gushing more about his black leather skinnies than his sensational halfpipe. "I *wanted* to look like a rock star out there," he cheerfully admitted. Do you think that other muscle-toned stars like Madonna ever forget aesthetics when engaged in athletics? No way. Whether jogging in spandex or riding in style, Madonna and her horse have even been known to go matchy-matchy. Whoa!

Good sports
(Clockwise from above) Victoria Beckham on the slopes; Fergie out for a jog; tennista Anna Kournikova; Madonna rides a pony.

Wave runner
Model/surfer
Tori Praver, no
stranger to the
life amphibious,
pairs a sleek swim
suit with draped
skirt.

Pulling it Together

Easy-to-wear pieces in delicious fabrics are fashion's answer to comfort food.

F CITY DRESSING TAKES ITS CUES from the street, then country chic makes nature its muse. For warm days, that translates into tropical florals, sun-kissed colors or seaworthy fabrics like cotton and canvas. Winter-worthy wear tends toward furs, trapper hats, whimsically patterned Nordic wools and lumberjack checks. Classic silhouettes fare better for outdoor activities than avant-garde shapes, extreme heels and heavy, high-maintenance jewelry. Hippie favorites like clogs are a country go-to, while organic fabrics have never looked more at one with nature.

ELEMENTS *of* STYLE

O'ER THE FIELDS YOU GO WITH THESE RUSTIC CHARMS. »

NEUTRAL COAT
While the quintessential urban palette starts and ends with black, country style takes inspiration from nature with shifting tones of sand, stone, ivory.

1

CRISP KHAKIS
Like jeans with a military training, the classic staple can be dressed up with sequins or toughed up with combat boots.

2

ETHNIC SATCHEL Brainy global nomads love the bookbag shape and durable folkloric fabric pattern.

3

TORTOISE SHADES In the race for most classic shades pattern, tortoise shell—sported by everyone from JFK to Mary Kate Olsen—always wins.

4

PREPPY RIBBON BELT Old-school stripes with brass fittings and sturdy grosgrain ribbon cinch the deal.

5

Signature Style

"**P**OWER UP your country weekend look with a little irreverent energy," says Michal Kors (pictured above). "Think sexy silk pajama pants with a posh, preppy cashmere turtleneck and a giant fur messenger bag that transforms what is normally a workaday look into a genius indulgence. I've always loved to see just how the world's great fashion icons have so skillfully broken fashion's rules. Like cheeky Kate Moss in a tiny mini dress and big rubber Hunter boots at a muddy outdoor rock concert in England. Instantly iconic. It's not always easy to find something that's utilitarian, glamorous and makes you smile all at once, but I think my neon fur trapper hats do all that. Needless to say, Day-Glo pinks, oranges and greens instantly lift the spirits on a gray frigid day. That said, for weekends out of the city, nothing says laid-back luxe like camel. After a work week spent in black and gray, embracing a light-toned neutral color found in nature is, I truly believe, healthy and bracing. It's also great for packing, as it's a perfect accent color that mixes well with white cottons and linens, gray sweats and of course lived-in denim."

Country code
Michael Kors (top right) citifies classic rustic looks. (Clockwise from top left) Silk pj pants with turtleneck; trapper hat in neon fur; camel leather adds luxe to a gray T; Kate Moss dresses up rubber wellies; stylized riding boot; Fergie makes an entrance with a shiny white MK tote.

"I think every stylish woman looks at Kate Moss and says, 'Now, why didn't I wear wellies with a dress?'"

MICHAEL KORS

Au Naturel Hair

Nude Lips

Deal Makers

Minimalist designer Calvin Klein once quipped, "Natural is best, but it takes makeup to look natural." (One or two other things don't hurt, either.)

Rain Gear

Dewy Skin

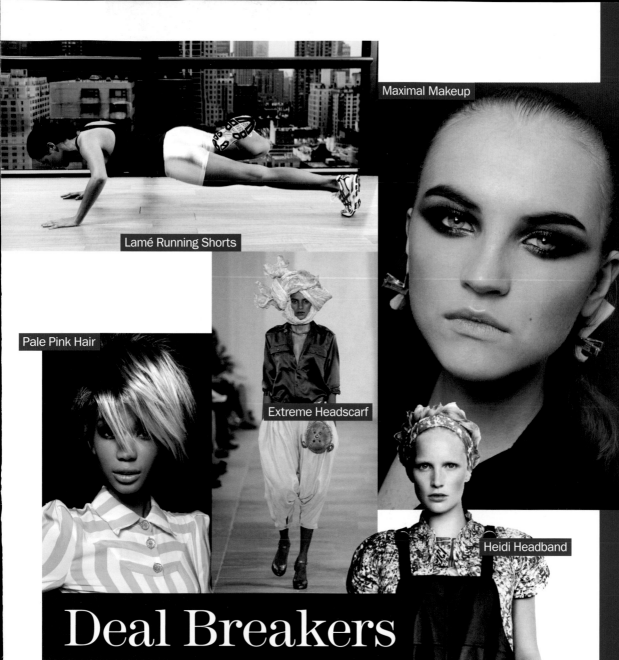

Maximal Makeup

Lamé Running Shorts

Pale Pink Hair

Extreme Headscarf

Heidi Headband

Deal Breakers

Don't try to fool Mother Nature with artificial hues, faux fabrics or glitzy trends.

157

Good Footing

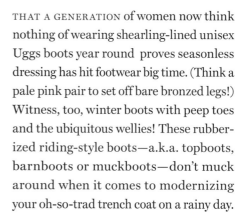

THAT A GENERATION of women now think nothing of wearing shearling-lined unisex Uggs boots year round proves seasonless dressing has hit footwear big time. (Think a pale pink pair to set off bare bronzed legs!) Witness, too, winter boots with peep toes and the ubiquitous wellies! These rubberized riding-style boots—a.k.a. topboots, barnboots or muckboots—don't muck around when it comes to modernizing your oh-so-trad trench coat on a rainy day.

INVEST IN

❏ A sturdy shearling boot in black or neutral with shiny embellishments.

❏ Rubber boots with refined details like croc embossing or metal buckles.

❏ Utilitarian boots with a heel for urban days and posh dinners in the country.

❏ A safari hat worn seductively low that plays off sequin harem pants.

❏ A flirty fur-trimmed hood that romanticizes an olive drab Army parka.

❏ An airy perforated brim to keep you cool and add to your mysterious allure.

THERE'S AN ALL-AMERICAN pragmatism and pride in our relationship with hats. Just look how we've exported the humble baseball cap as a global symbol of nonchalance and cool—while keeping the sun out of our eyes and rain off our faces. For femme fatales in fedoras as well as trendistas in fur trappers, the perfect hat shows off a self-awareness that's gutsy and glam all at once.

Heady Stuff

CHAPTER NINE

Dressing for...

Great Escapes

Fun In The Sun Style

VACATION CHIC SHOULD be escapist—off the charts with sun-drenched colors, see-through fabrics and Caribbean Carnival–worthy sandals. In a lush locale, zipping a bright blue biker jacket over a bikini and hitting a Tiki Bar isn't taboo, but acceptably addictive. Designers never seem to get over their incurable crush on the original suntanned siren jet–setter like Grace Kelly in cat–eye shades and paisley tunics, or bronzed, bejeweled Liz Taylor in a floor-length pink and green caftan. Says Tina Bossidy, designer of the Samba Soleil line, "It's no wonder the '60s sand–grazing caftan became a beach classic; it's more forgiving than the bikini. Regal and roomy, slip one on and feel like a queen."

"I really want to give women this sense of freedom."

PHOEBE PHILO, CREATIVE DIRECTOR, CELINE

PLAYLIST »

Ticket to paradise? Resort classics in tropical hues, tricked out with exquisite exotica.

■ **Classic caftan**
The jet–setter's staple from Palm Beach to Positano, its loose fit and long length adds to its allure and versatility. (1)

■ **Cool cover-up**
Make free with fierce urban elements—yup, a biker jacket and boots at a beach resort—and earn street cred even on the boardwalk. (2)

■ **White trousers**
The undeniable truth: You shouldn't leave home without a perfect pair of white pants (whether wide or skinny). The #1 summer wardrobe staple. (3)

■ **Sheer dress**
To tunic or not to tunic? Find a sheer one and you've got yourself a bikini cover–up, a companion to leggings, a light layer to tuck under a shawl. (4)

■ **Sexy sandal**
Nothing neutral about them: A wildly exotic sandal gains you insta-access to VIP clubs. Let's get this beach party started! (5)

■ **Tropical bag**
No greater buzz kill than having to lug around a back-breaking bag when you're traveling; think cute, color-happy and accommodating. (6)

1

2

3

4

5

6

Some like it hot
First-class chic no
matter what your ticket
says (at right): multi-
striped tango dress.
Opposite: bikini top
with blazer; graphic mix
with vibrant green tote;
tropic-colorful top with
comfy black pants.

Fantastic Voyage

*Travel looks that reflect
your destination
guarantee a mood lift—
and an upgrade!*

NOTHING WRONG with
making a splash before you
get to your vacation spot.
Choose an en-route look in
the same "key" as your glam getaway:
a sleek tropical print T, a slick scuba-
inspired top, maybe a ruffled rumba
skirt. Feeling the vibe of a place is the
next best thing to being there. And
you don't have to fly first class to feel
pampered: Treat yourself to "comfort
fashion" like fab flats in luxe leathers,
fabrics that breathe and feel dreamy
against bare skin. A ravishing, roomy
bright-colored carry-on will always
cheer you up—even during a long
flight delay!

"FASHION MUST BE AN INTOXICATING RELEASE FROM THE BANALITY OF THE WORLD."

—Diana Vreeland, 20th-century American style icon, editor, museum curator

Rich Beach

Given our addiction to seasonless style, we love a cocktail of swimwear mixed with street wear.

CALL IT SOLAR OPPOSITES: beach fashion that flaunts a sophisticated streak. Unorthodox pairing of daywear skirts and bikini tops, precious beach totes and a pirate's trove of shiny trinkets: It's what lets you slip off the beach and into a booth at a chic café for lunch as fast as your platform espadrilles can get you there.

Siren call
Mad sexy au soleil (clockwise from above) ladylike bikini suit; prints with a pirate's booty of bling; bandeau top with maxi skirt; see-through cover-up; goddess-style pleated maillot; print chiffon caftan with matching bikini; sailor striped blazer and matching bikini.

Walking on sunshine Ship-to-shore chic merges ladylike tops and bags with bikini bottoms.

Star Trippers…
Guess Who?!

Topping fashion's heat index: A-listers at glam getaways.

WHEN THE STARS COME OUT to play can the paparazzi be far behind? Not likely. Which is why celebs no longer save their best fashion efforts for the red carpet. Fans and photogs eagerly anticipate what their idols will look like in "less"— bikinis, see-through sarongs or micro-sized cutoffs. And while stars can run, they can't hide: If they're skimping on gym visits or sporting a new boyfriend as arm candy, the news will break on their beach holiday!

Sunny lady
Royal navy, anyone? From left to right: Kate Middleton in sailor stripes; Catherine Zeta Jones in black and gold; Sienna Miller matches straw fedora and tote; Chanel Iman in groovy paisley tunic.

Made in the shades
Victoria Beckham tricks out a one-sleeved trench with leopard bikini and retro-style bescarfed bouffant.

Pulling it Together

Dream vacations call for fantasy looks: Indulge in tropical hues, revealing cuts and sensuous fabrics.

BETWEEN THE FAR-FLUNG cultural references (Morocco, Tahiti, St Tropez, Palm Beach) and eye-popping color palette, vacation fashion is a feast for the senses. By all means, indulge yourself now because exotic fare like sheer ruffled palazzo pants, tangerine-colored leather and chunky sun-reflecting chokers generally don't fly in the office. Still, there's method to the madness of getaway glam: If you're going with a magenta tank, offset it with a neutral skirt, or prep out provocatively short micro shorts with a snug blazer. Invited for a cocktail après-surf? Make sure you've stashed your thigh-high boots in the dune buggy and you're good to go. Bottoms up!

ELEMENTS *of* STYLE

LUXE LOOT FINDS ITS PLACE IN THE SUN.

SNAKESKIN ESPADRILLES The Spanish-born, rope-soled staple scales new heights.

1

MAD MÉLANGE Looking like you raided the islander gift shop is the whole point.

2

Signature Style

WHETHER OR NOT your getaway is one where you're giving back—and there is no shortage of opportunities for 'voluntourism' these days—you can reduce your carbon footprint with eco-friendly fashion choices," says Amanda Hearst, associate market editor for *Marie Claire* (pictured above). "Look for the increasing number of good-karma designers who work with reclaimed textiles or sustainable materials, many donating part of their profits to environmental causes or sourcing their natural clothing and accessories from indigenous crafts people." Often these 'green facts' appear on the brands' websites—so read them! Even if you don't make it to Nepal to help repair roads and trails, you can still show solidarity wearing a locally crafted necklace pendant of bone etched with Tibetan symbols or sunglasses of recycled stainless steel. Wouldn't it make sense to sport a sweet little sundress made of reclaimed antique linens with real cherry stones as buttons if you're all for rainforest conservation? Organic cotton T-shirts and vegan knapsacks made from recycled plastic water bottles are an excellent choice for someone pitching in with marine conservation. "Whenever we support ethical fashion, we help reduce poverty and environmental damage," says Hearst. "You can always find conservation-minded carryalls—like those canvas totes that support the Wayuu Taya Foundation to benefit indigenous Latin-American communities. Sweet smell of ethical success? A delicious designer fragrance that's also sustainable. Our fashion choices have an impact."

Survival of the chicest

(From top to bottom) Charmingly mismatched bikini of recycled textiles; vegan tote; bangles made of woolly mammoth tusk fossils; bateau-striped top in organic, carbon-neutral cotton; a turquoise diamond ring made from recycled stones; lavender recycled suede mocs.

66 You can be just
as chic in necklaces
of beads handmade
in Rwanda and
sandals created
sustainably from
start to finish
in California."

AMANDA HEARST

Deal Makers

Now's the time to use ocean spray as hairspray, get a temporary tattoo, lacquer up the nails with lime green!

Brimming with Chic

Neutral Palette

Lime Aid

Tat's All, Folks

Ocean Waves

Too Perfect for La Plage

Overshadowed!

Deal Breakers

High and Dry

Why sport anything that would prevent you from plunging into the sea or playing a vigorous game of beach volleyball?

Kiss of Death

Bling Overload

Hot to Handle

DIANA VREELAND'S FAMOUS observation that "Pink is the navy blue of India" meant to convey that the various shades of fuchsia, peony and magenta are the "everyday" standard in sultry places just as dark tones are in Northern climes. So it stands to reason that the bag you tote on a sunny holiday blends in with the flora, fauna and alfresco fun!

INVEST IN

❏ A bright-toned python bag you'll bequeath to your daughter or godchild.

❏ A sturdy straw or rattan tote, for tradition's sake.

❏ A ravishing, roomy woven carryall that works for weekends and plane travel.

Treasure Principle

STEADY, PIRATE QUEENS: The new species of glittery global bling is too fabulous to confine to a deserted isle. Designers have been trolling the ocean, garden and—obviously—buried treasure for shiny finery fierce enough for Captain Jack Sparrow.

INVEST IN

❏ Classic cameos and spiritual amulets to attract attention and ward off evil spirits.

❏ Skull symbols are equally "to die" for in a pirate's cove, Goth club or Ivy League fraternity.

❏ "Sustainable" trinkets of stone, wood and bone are naturally nifty and exotic.

Index

Accessories. *See* specific accessories
Aniston, Jennifer, 58, 59, 76

Bags and totes
    for city weekends, 127, 141
    for clubs/concerts, 96–97, 105
    for cocktail parties/black tie, 71, 79, 85
    for country weekends, 145, 153, 154
    for dates, 53, 61, 66
    for day to night, 35, 46
    for great escapes, 163, 164, 168, 172, 176
    for job interviews, 13, 19, 20, 22, 30
    for official functions, 109, 112
Bailey, Christopher, 136–137
Basinger, Kim, 76
Beach attire, 166–167.
    See also Great escapes
Beckham, Victoria, 114, 150, 169
Beyoncé, 98, 99, 100
Black tie. *See* Cocktail parties/black tie
Bogner, Willy, 146
Brown, Foxy, 116
Bruni, Carla, 18, 19
Buccini, Beth, 42
Burton, Sarah, 100–101

Caftans, 162, 163, 166, 171
Campbell, Naomi, 116
Chanel, Coco, 31, 95
City weekends, 124–141
    about: overview of looks, 126–127
    accessories for. *See* specific accessories
    biker style, 130–131, 134, 136, 140
    coat styles, 127, 128, 136
    deal makers and breakers, 138–139
    divas in distressed, 132–133
    elements of style, 134–135
    hairstyles, 138, 139
    pants styles, 129, 130–133, 135
    playlist, 127
    shoe styles, 127, 135, 136, 138, 139, 140
    signature style (Bailey), 136–137
    uptown express, 128–129
    urban playdate, 130–135

Cleavage, 23, 118
Clinton, Hillary, 20
Clubs and concerts, 86–105
    about: overview of looks, 88–89
    accessories for. *See* specific accessories
    coat styles, 90
    country style, 94–97
    deal makers and breakers, 102–103
    diva style, 98–99
    elements of style, 92–93, 96–97
    fabrics for, 89
    hairstyles, 102, 103
    jackets and blazers for, 89, 90, 91, 93
    pants styles, 89, 92, 95
    playlist, 89
    rock style, 90–93, 98–99
    shoe styles, 89, 91, 92, 93, 96, 103
    signature style (Burton), 100–101
Coats and capes
    for city weekends, 127, 128, 136
    for clubs/concerts, 90
    for cocktail parties/black tie, 74
    for country weekends, 145, 146–147, 152
    for day to night, 35
    for job interviews, 18, 27
    for official functions,
        109, 110–113, 118, 119
Cocktail parties/black tie, 68–85
    about: overview of looks, 70–71
    accessories for. *See* specific accessories
    black tie dressing, 76–79
    coat styles, 74
    cocktail party options, 72–75
    deal makers and breakers, 82–83
    dress styles, 71, 72, 74–79, 80
    elements of style, 74–75, 78–79
    hairstyles, 82, 83
    pants styles, 72, 73
    playlist, 71
    red carpet hits and misses, 76–77
    shoe styles, 71, 75, 79, 85
    signature style (Wang), 80–81
Coppola, Sofia, 58, 59
Country weekends, 142–159
    about: overview of looks, 144–145
    accessories for. *See* specific accessories
    athletic chic, 148–149

coat styles, 145, 146–147, 152
deal makers and breakers, 156–157
easy-to-wear pieces, 152–153
elements of style, 152–153
hairstyles, 156, 157
jock tactics, 150–151
pants styles, 146, 147, 154, 159
playlist, 145
shoe styles, 145, 148, 158
signature style (Kors), 154–155
Courtroom fashion, 116–117
Cover-ups, 67, 163, 166

Dates, 50–67
    about: overview of looks, 52–53
    accessories for. *See* specific accessories
    deal makers and breakers, 64–65
    demure "dress-up," 54–55
    dress styles, 56–61, 62
    elements of style, 60–61
    hot-night theme options, 60–61
    LBDs for, 58–59
    lingerie and, 53, 64, 65, 67
    passion statements, 56–57
    playlist, 53
    shoe styles, 53, 60
    signature style (Versace), 62–63
Day to night, 32–49
    about: overview of looks, 34–35
    accessories for. *See* specific accessories
    coat or cape for, 35
    daring to bare skin, 48–49
    deal makers and breakers, 44–45
    dress styles, 35, 38–39
    elements of style, 40–41
    fabrics, 35, 36, 37
    hairstyles, 44, 45
    looks that work and play, 36–37
    pants styles, 42
    playlist, 35
    serious but sexy balance, 40–41
    shoe styles, 35, 40, 44
    signature style (Easley and
        Buccini), 42–43
Deal makers and breakers
    for city weekends, 138–139
    for clubs/concerts, 102–103

for cocktail parties/black tie, 82–83
for country weekends, 156–157
for dates, 64–65
for day to night, 44–45
for great escapes, 174–175
for job interviews, 22–23
for official functions, 120–121
Dello Russo, Anna, 118
Designers. *See* Signature style
Dresses
    for clubs/concerts. *See* Clubs
      and concerts
    for cocktail parties/black
      tie, 71, 72, 74–79, 80
    for dates, 56–61, 62
    for day to night, 35, 38–39
    LBDs, 58–59
    for official functions, 109

Easley, Sarah, 42–43
Elements of style
    black tie, 78–79
    city weekends, 134–135
    clubs/concerts, 92–93, 96–97
    cocktail parties, 74–75
    country weekends, 152–153
    dates, 60–61
    day to night, 40–41
    great escapes, 170–171
    job interviews, 18–19, 26–27
    official functions, 112–113

Fergie, 150, 154
Ford, Tom, 88
Funerals and weddings, 114–115

Gaga, Lady, 98
Ghesquière, Nicolas, 55
Glasses and shades, 74, 89, 93, 113,
    135, 138, 153, 171
Gloves, 44, 61, 115, 123
Goldberg, Whoopie, 76
Great escapes, 160–177
    about: overview of looks, 162–163
    accessories for. *See* specific accessories
    beach attire, 166–167
    caftans and, 162, 163, 166, 171

celeb fashion, 168–169
deal makers and breakers, 174–175
elements of style, 170–171
hairstyles, 174, 175
pants styles, 163, 164, 165, 170
playlist, 163
shoe styles, 163, 170, 171
signature style (Hearst), 172–173
travel attire, 164–165
tunics and, 163, 168
Gunn, Tim, 118–119

Hairstyles
    for city weekends, 138, 139
    for clubs/concerts, 102, 103
    for cocktail parties/black tie, 82, 83
    for country weekends, 156, 157
    for dates, 65
    for day to night, 44, 45
    for great escapes, 174, 175
    for job interviews, 22, 23
    for official functions, 120, 121
Handbags. *See* Bags and totes
Harry, Debbie, 92
Hats
    for country weekends, 145, 154, 159
    for job interviews, 27
    for official functions, 113, 118, 121, 122
Hearst, Amanda, 172–173
Hendricks, Christina, 59
Hepburn, Katharine, 17
Holmes, Katie, 132
Hynde, Chryssie, 92

Iman, Chanel, 168

Jackets and blazers. *See*
    also Coats and capes
    for bikini cover-up, 162, 163
    for city weekends, 130, 132, 134, 136
    for clubs/concerts, 89, 90, 91, 93
    for cocktail parties/black tie, 80
    for country weekends, 146
    for dates, 56, 67
    for day to night, 36–37, 49
    for great escapes, 165, 166, 170
    for job interviews, 13, 24, 26

Jacobs, Marc, 70
Jewelry
    for city weekends, 127, 139
    for clubs/concerts, 89, 91, 92, 97,
      102, 103, 104
    for cocktail parties/black tie, 71, 75,
      78–79, 84
    for dates, 53, 61
    for day to night, 35, 41, 42, 45, 47
    for great escapes, 175, 177
    for job interviews, 19, 31
    for official functions, 109, 113, 122
Job interviews, 10–31
    about: overview of looks, 12–13
    accessories for. *See* specific accessories
    coat styles, 18, 27
    corporate look, 14, 16–19
    creative look, 14, 24–27
    deal makers and breakers, 22–23
    elements of style, 18–19, 26–27
    hairstyles, 22, 23
    playlist, 13
    shoe styles, 13, 18, 23, 26, 27, 28–29
    signature style (Karan), 20–21
Johnson, Samuel, 111
Jolie, Angelina, 17

Karan, Donna, 20–21
Kidman, Nicole, 58, 59
Klein, Ann, 20
Klein, Calvin, 126, 156
Klum, Heidi, 100
Kors, Michael, 129, 154–155
Kournikova, Anna, 150

Lauren, Ralph, 144
Lingerie and stockings, 53, 64, 65, 67, 82
Lohan, Lindsay, 116
Lopez, Jennifer, 62
Loren, Sophia, 52

Madonna, 62, 88, 98, 150
Makeup
    for city weekends, 138, 139
    for clubs/concerts, 102, 103
    for cocktail parties/black tie, 82, 83
    for country weekends, 156, 157

for dates, 64, 65, 66
for great escapes, 174, 175
for job interviews, 22, 23
for official functions, 120
McCartney, Stella, 72
McQueen, Alexander, 100, 114
Mendes, Eva, 76
Middleton, Kate, 100, 118, 122, 168
Middleton, Pippa, 114
Miller, Sienna, 168
Mizrahi, Isaac, 26
Moore, Demi, 76
Moore, Mandy, 133
Moss, Kate, 114, 154, 155

Obama, Michelle, 18, 19
Official functions, 106–123
   about: overview of looks, 108–109
   accessories for. *See* specific accessories
   coat styles, 109, 110–113, 118, 119
   courtroom fashion, 116–117
   deal makers and breakers, 120–121
   dress styles, 109
   elements of style, 112–113
   hairstyles, 120, 121
   playlist, 109
   shoe styles, 109, 121
   signature style (Gunn), 118–119
   weddings and funerals, 114–115

Paltrow, Gwyneth, 70
Pants
   for city weekends, 129, 130–133, 135
   for clubs/concerts, 89, 92, 95
   for cocktail parties/black tie, 72, 73
   for country weekends, 146, 147,
      154, 159
   for day to night, 42
   for great escapes, 163, 164, 165, 170
Pantsuits, 18, 20, 24, 40, 100, 101
Perry, Katy, 90
Philo, Phoebe, 162
Playlists
   city weekends, 127
   clubs/concerts, 89
   cocktail parties/black tie, 71
   country weekends, 145

date, 53
day to night, 35
great escapes, 163
job interview, 13
official functions, 109
Prada, Miuccia, 37
Praver, Tori, 151

Rassi, Zanna Roberts, 15
Richards, Alexandra, 90
Rihanna, 98, 132
Rogers, Millicent, 96
Russell, Rosalind, 17
Ryder, Winona, 116

Saint Laurent, Yves, 34
Sanders, Jil, 114
Shades. *See* Glasses and shades
Shields, Brooke, 58, 59
Shoes
   for city weekends, 127, 135, 136,
      138, 139, 140
   for clubs/concerts, 89, 91, 92, 93,
      96, 103
   for cocktail parties/black tie, 71,
      75, 79, 85
   for country weekends, 145, 148, 158
   for dates, 53, 60
   for day to night, 35, 40, 44
   for great escapes, 163, 170, 171
   for job interviews, 13,
      18, 23, 26, 27, 28–29
   for official functions, 109, 121
Signature style
   Bailey, Christopher, 136–137
   Buccini, Beth, and
      Easley, Sarah, 42–43
   Burton, Sarah, 100–101
   Easley, Sarah, and
      Buccini, Beth, 42–43
   Gunn, Tim, 118–119
   Hearst, Amanda, 172–173
   Karan, Donna, 20–21
   Kors, Michael, 154–155
   Versace, Donatella, 62–63
   Wang, Vera, 80–81
Simpson, Jessica, 76, 172

Skin, showing, 48–49, 63, 147, 149
Suits. *See also* Pantsuits
   for job interviews, 13, 15, 16–19, 20,
      24–25, 26–27
   for official functions, 117, 118
Swank, Hillary, 77
Swift, Taylor, 95

Tatou, Audrey, 16, 17
Tiaras and headbands, 78, 92, 112, 157
Tomlin, Lily, 10
Travel attire. *See* Great escapes

Versace, Donatella, 62–63
Vests, 90, 130, 145, 148
Vreeland, Diana, 60, 165, 176

Wang, Vera, 40, 80–81
Wasson, Erin, 132
Watches, 13, 18, 31, 41
Watson, Emma, 81, 136
Weddings and funerals, 114–115
Weekends. *See* City weekends;
   Country weekends
Wilde, Oscar, 108
Williams, Victoria, 80
Wilson, Gretchen, 95
Windsor, Lady Frederick, 118
Witherspoon, Reese, 17, 76

Zeta Jones, Catherine, 168

Photo Credits

Cover David Oldham (jean outfit) OR Richard Bailey (white trench coat)
P14-15 Joanna Coles
From left: Courtesy of the Style Network; Dan Lecca
P16-17 Nina Garcia
From left: Barbara Nitke/Bravo; Rankin

CHAPTER 1
P10 Joshua Jordan
P12-13 Clockwise from left: Ben Watts; Dan Lecca (5); Ben Goldstein/Studio D
P14-15 From left: Neil Kirk; Dan Lecca (3)
P16-17 From left: Chantal Thomine-Desmazures/Haut et Court/Cine@/The Kobal Collection; Underwood & Underwood/Corbis; Clarence Sinclair Bull/John Kobal Foundation/Getty Images; Sam Emerson/MGM/The Kobal Collection; Marcel Thomas/FilmMagic.com
P18-19 Clockwise from top left: Dan Lecca (7); Emmanuel Dunand/AFP/Getty Images; Jesus Ayala/Studio D; Jemal Countess/WireImage.com; Richard Pierce; Ben Goldstein/Studio D
P20-21 Clockwise from top left: Dan Lecca (2); Stuart Tyson/Studio D; Courtesy of Donna Karan; Mark Van Holden/WireImage.com; Joshua Jordan; Courtesy of Donna Karan (2); Dan Lecca; Guilio Marocchi/SIPA
P22-23 Clockwise from top left: GoRunway.com; Patric Shaw; Tesh; Richard Pierce; Fabio Pettinari; Dan Lecca; Matt Jones; Jeffrey Westbrook/Studio D; Mei Tao; Tesh
P24-25 Clockwise from top left: Firstview.com; Dan Lecca (3); Neil Kirk; Dan Lecca; Neil Kirk; Matt Jones
P26-27 Clockwise from top left: Dan Lecca (7); Courtesy of Rochas; Dan Lecca; Marcus Mam; Dan Lecca; Richard Pierce

P28-29 Clockwise from top left: Charlotte Jenks Lewis/Studio D; Ben Goldstein/Studio D; James Macari; Simon Burstall; Ben Goldstein/Studio D; David Oldham; Richard Majchrzak/Studio D; Charlotte Jenks Lewis/Studio D; Ben Goldstein/Studio D; Courtesy of Tory Burch; Ben Goldstein/Studio D (2)
P30-31 Clockwise from top left: Joshua Jordan; Matt Jones; Ben Goldstein/Studio D; Jeffrey Westbrook/Studio D; Richard Pierce; Charlotte Jenks Lewis/Sudio D; Ben Goldstein/Studio D

CHAPTER 2
P32 Kalle Gustafsson
P34-35 Clockwise from left: Ben Watts; Courtesy of Chris Benz; Dan Lecca (2); Ben Goldstein/Studio D (3)
P36-37 Clockwise from left: Marcus Mam; Courtesy of Malo; Dan Lecca; Greg Kessler
P38-39 Clockwise from top left: Imaxtree.com; Ruven Afanador; Txema Yeste; Dan Lecca, Marcus Mam; Bill Diodato; Mel Karch
P40-41 Clockwise from top left: Dan Lecca (7); Mary Rozzi; Jeff Harris; Charlotte Jenks Lewis/Studio D; Jeff Harris (2)
P42-43 Clockwise from top left: Dan Lecca; Ben Goldstein/Studio D; Douglas Friedman; Ben Watts; Ben Goldstein/Studio D (2); Courtesy of KirnaZabete.com; Ben Goldstein/Studio D
P44-45 Clockwise from top left: Ilan Rubin; Ben Goldstein/Studio D; Greg Kessler; Dan Lecca (2); Capra/Mondadori Syndication; Matt Jones; Courtesy of YSL; Ruven Afanador
P46-47 Clockwise from top left: David Roemer; Charlotte Jenks Lewis/Studio D; Kevin Sinclair; Ben Goldstein/Studio D; (2); Charlotte Jenks Lewis/Stuiod D; Ben Watts; Jeff Harris

P48-49 Clockwise from top left: Greg Kessler; David Oldham (2); Kevin Sinclair; Tesh; Jeff Harris; Dan Lecca

CHAPTER 3
P50 Jonty Davies
P52-53 Clockwise from left: Neil Kirk; Jeffrey Westbrook/Studio D; Dan Lecca (2); Jeffrey Westbrook/Studio D; Jeff Harris; Ben Goldstein/Studio D
P54-55 From left: David Oldham; Dan Lecca (3)
P56-57 Clockwise from top left: Kayt Jones; Dan Lecca (4); Neil Kirk; Kevin Sinclair; David Roemer; Kevin Sinclair
P58-59 From left: James Devanet/WireImage.com; Kevin Mazur/WireImage.com; John Sciulli/WireImage.com; Reuters/Corbis; Perry Hagopian
P60-61 Clockwise from top left: Dan Lecca (7); Courtesy of Mawi; Philip Gay; Richard Pierce; Dan Lecca; Ben Goldstein/Studio D
P62-63 Clockwise from top left: Dan Lecca; Jeffrey Westbrook/Studio D; Charles Eshelman/FilmMagic.com; James Macari; Frank Micelotta/FOX/PictureGroup via AP Images; Ben Goldstein/Studio D
P64-65 Clockwise from top left: Kelly Klein; Max Cardelli; Ben Watts; David Roemer; Dan Lecca; Max Cardelli; Pamela Hanson/TrunkArchive.com (2); Scott & Zoe; Kariv/Mandadori Syndication
P66-67 Clockwise from left: Ben Watts; Richard Pierce; Fabio Chizzola; Ben Goldstein/Studio D (5); Jeffrey Westbrook/Studio D (2); Charlotte Jenks Lewis/Studio D; David Roemer

CHAPTER 4
P68 Kayt Jones
P70-71 Clockwise from left: David Oldham; Dan Lecca; Ben Goldstein/Studio D; Greg Kessler; Will Whipple/

Guardian News + Media LTD 2011; Firstview.com; Ben Goldstein/Studio D

P72-73 Clockwise from top left: Neil Kirk; David Roemer; Greg Kessler; Courtesy of Stella McCartney; David Oldham; Jason Lloyd Evans; Pamela Hanson

P74-75 Clockwise from top left: Dan Lecca (7); Franck Dieleman; Ben Goldstein/Studio D; Jeffrey Westbrook/Studio D; Ben Goldstein/Studio D (2)

P76-77 Clockwise from top left: Jim Smeal/WireImage.com; Jeff Kravitz/FilmMagic.com; Angela Weiss/WireImage.com; Richard Bailey; Steve Granitz/WireImage.com; Reed Saxon/AP Photo; Evan Agostini/Getty Images; Trapper Frank/Sygma/Corbis

P78-79 Clockwise from top left: Dan Lecca (2); Iris Brosch; Dan Lecca (3); Firstview.com; Charlotte Jenks Lewis/Studio D; Dan Lecca (2); Ben Goldstein/Studio D; Pamela Hanson

P80-81 Clockwise from top left: Dan Lecca; Courtesy of Vera Wang; D. Dipasupil/FilmMagic.com; Tesh; Kevin Mazur/WireImage.com; Courtesy of Vera Wang; Dan Lecca

P82-83 Clockwise from top left: Ruven Afanador; Studio D (2); Guy Aroch; George Chan; Dan Lecca (2); Fabio Pettinari; Francois Nars; Ruven Afanador; Andrew Durham

P84-85 Clockwise from top left: Jem Mitchell; Ben Goldstein/Studio D; Jody Doyle; Ray Kachatorian; Ben Goldstein/Studio D; Jeff Harris; Stuart Tyson/Studio D (2); Richard Pierce; Lara Robby/Studio D; Ben Goldstein/Studio D

CHAPTER 5

P86 David Roemer

P88-89 Clockwise from left: Tesh; Ben Goldstein/Studio D; Dan Lecca (2); Ben Goldstein/Studio D (2); Courtesy of Roberto Cavalli

P90-91 Clockwise from top left: Bryan Adams; Dan Lecca; David Oldham; David Roemer; Junko Kimura/Getty Images; Dan Lecca; C Polk/Getty Images; James Macari; Bryan Adams; Derek Kettela

P92-93 Clockwise from top left: Dan Lecca (7); Charlotte Jenks Lewis/Studio D; Firstview.com; Ben Goldstein /Studio D; Charlotte Jenks Lewis/Studio D; Ben Goldstein/Studio D

P94-95 From left: Greg Kessler; Fabio Chizzola; Dan Lecca (2)

P96-97 Clockwise from top left: Dan Lecca (3); Greg Kessler; Dan Lecca; David Roemer; Dan Lecca; Courtesy of Zac Posen; Charlotte Jenks Lewis/Studio D; Courtesy of Ralph Lauren; Charlotte Jenks Lewis/Studio D Ben Goldstein/Studio D (3)

P98-99 Clockwise from top left: Fotonoticias/WireImage.com; Christopher Polk/Getty Images; Peggy Sirota; Mark Healy; PacificCoastNews.com; Celebrity Photo

P100-101 Clockwise from top left: Splash News; Venturelli/WireImage.com; Dave M. Benett/Getty Images; Dan Lecca (2); Ben Goldstein/Studio D; Diego Fuga

P102-103 Clockwise from top left: Peggy Sirota; Simon Burstall; Dan Lecca (2); Richard Pierce; Fabio Chizzola; Jeffrey Westbrook/Studio D; Tesh; David Oldham; Greg Kessler

P104-105 Clockwise ftom top left: Matt Jones; Ben Goldstein/Studio D; Stuart Tyson/Studio D; Ben Goldstein/Studio D (2); Richard Pierce; David Oldham; Stuart Tyson/Studio D; Patric Shaw; Ben Goldstein/Studio D

CHAPTER 6

P106 David Ferrua

P108-109 Clockwise from left: Courtesy of Chanel; Marcus Mam; Charlotte Jenks Lewis/Studio D; Ben Goldstein/Studio D (2); Dan Lecca; Firstview.com

P110-111 From left: Ruven Afanador; Dan Lecca; Imaxtree.com; Dan Lecca

P112-113 Clockwise from top left: Dan Lecca (8); Charlotte Jenks Lewis/Studio D; Ben Goldstein/Studio D; Jeff Harris; Charlotte Jenks Lewis/Studio D

P114-115 Clockwise from top left: PacificCoastNews.com (2); Jason Lloyd Evans; Danny Martindale/FilmMagic.com; Mirrorpix/Splash News; Fabio Chizzola; Raphael Mazzucco; Mike Marsland/WireImage.com

P116-117 Clockwise from top left: Jim Ruymen/Reuters; Reuters; David Tonnessen/PacificCoastNews.com; Dan Lecca; Gregory P. Mango/Splash News

P118-119 Clockwise from top left: Dan Lecca; Dimitrios Kambouris/WireImage.com; Txema Yste; Andrew Durham; Lionel Cironneau/AP Photo; Chris Jackson/Getty Images; Dan Lecca

P120-121 Clockwise from top left: Fabio Chizzola; Greg Delves; Ralph Mecke; Marcus Mam; Neil Kirk; Dan Lecca; Ben Goldstein/Studio D; Diego Fuga; Greg Kessler; Mary Rozzi

P122-123 Clockwise from bottom left: Jacopo Raule/Getty Images; Danny Martindale/FilmMagic.com; Indigo/Getty Images; Simon Burstall; Firstview.com; Simon Burstall; James Macari

CHAPTER 7

P124 David Oldham

P216-127 Clockwise from left: Patric Shaw; Andrew McLeod; Dan Lecca (2); Jeffrey Westbrook/Studio D; Richard Pierce; Ben Goldstein/Studio D

P128-129 From left: Kevin Sinclair; Dan Lecca (3)

P130-131 Clockwise from top left: David

Oldham; Ruven Afanador; Peggy Sirota; Dan Lecca; James Macari; Dan Lecca; David Roemer; Dan Lecca

P132-133 From left: J. Lowery/Startraksphoto.com; James Devaney/WireImage.com; Chris Radcliffe/BauerGriffin.com; James White

P134-135 Clockwise from top left: Dan Lecca (2); Firstview.com; Dan Lecca (4); Andrew McLeod; Ben Goldstein/Studio D (4)

P136-137 Clockwise from top left: PacificCoastNews.com; Dan Lecca; Neil Kirk; Simon Burstall; Dan Lecca; Charlotte Jenks Lewis/Studio D; Jeffrey Westbrook/Studio D

P138-139 Clockwise from left: Dan Lecca; Jason Lloyd Evans; Richard Bailey; Ilan Rubin/TrunkArchive.com; TrunkArchive.com; James Macari; Dan Lecca; Simon Burstall; Tesh; Charlotte Jenks Lewis/Studio D

P140-141 Clockwise from top left: Simon Burstall; Richard Pierce; David Oldham; Ben Goldstein/Studio D; Ilan Rubin; Ben Goldstein/Studio D; Kevin Sinclair; Andrew McLeod; Dan Lecca; Imaxtree.com; Ben Goldstein/Studio D

CHAPTER 8

P142 Kayt Jones

P144-145 Clockwise from left: Yu Tsai; Dan Lecca (4); Andrew McLeod; Ilan Rubin

P146-147 Clockwise from top left: Ruven Afanador; Dan Lecca (3); Peggy Sirota; Dan Lecca; Kayt Jones; Guy Aroch

P148-149 From left: Matt Jones; Dan Lecca (3)

P150-151 Clockwise from left: Suu/Martines/Splash News; INFphoto.com; Matthew Stockman/Getty Images; Matt Jones; Barm/Fame Pictures

P152-153 Clockwise from top left: Dan Lecca; Firstview.com (2); Dan Lecca (3); Courtesy of the Gap; Curtis Hemmert/J.McLaughlin; Andrew McLeod (2); Dan Lecca (2)

P154-155 Clockwise from top left: Dan Lecca (2); Jason Kemplin/WireImage.com; Ben Watts; Dan Lecca; Matt Cardy/Getty Images; Charlotte Jenks Lewis/Studio D; Vickers/Kaminski/Splash News

P156-157 Clockwise from top left: sic/donja pitsch/helene roule; Jason Lloyd Evans; Ben Goldstein/Studio D; Greg Kessler; Peter Gehreke; Dan Lecca; Sean Cunningham; sic/frederic lucano/valerie masei; Carter Smith/Art + Commerce

P158-159 From left: Kayt Jones; Ben Goldstein/Studio D; Richard Pierce; Courtesy of El Vaquero; Dan Lecca; Simon Burstall; Tesh; Jeff Harris

CHAPTER 9

P160 James Macari

P162-163 Clockwise from left: Giles Bensimon; Dan Lecca (4); Charlotte Jenks Lewis/Studio D; Ilan Rubin

P164-165 From left: Txema Yeste; Dan Lecca; Courtesy of Proenza Schouler; Dan Lecca

P166-167 Clockwise from top left: Patric Shaw; Dan Lecca (3); David Oldham; Dan Lecca; Tesh; Ben Watts

P168-169 From Left: Splash News; Dominique Charriau/WireImage.com; Dan Bozinovski/Jason Green/BigPicturesPhoto.com; Vila/BauerGriffin; Ruven Afanador

P170-171 Clockwise from left: Dan Lecca (6); Firstview.com; Ben Goldstein/Studio D; Courtesy of Samba Soleil; Ben Goldstein/Studio D; Kalle Gustafsson; Richard Pierce

P172-173 Clockwise from top left: Dan Lecca; Ben Goldstein/Studio D; Jerritt Clark/WireImage.com; David Oldham; Ben Goldstein/Studio D (3); Stuart Tyson/Studio D

P174-175 Clockwise from top left: Matt Jones; James Macari; Jason Lloyd Evans; Dan Lecca; Greg Kessler; Bill Diodato; David Roemer; Jason Lloyd Evans; James Macari; Bill Diodato

P176-177 Clockwise from top left: Jeffrey Westbrook/Studio D; Ben Goldstein/Studio D; David Oldham; Richard Pierce; Ben Goldstein/Studio D; Yu Tsai; Andrew McLeod; Courtesy of Kate Spade

HEARST BOOKS
New York

An Imprint of Sterling Publishing
387 Park Avenue South
New York, NY 10016

Design by Michael Picón, minkwell.com
Cover Design by Michael Picón, minkwell.com

Library of Congress Cataloging-in-Publication Data

Corrigan, Joyce.
Marie Claire outfit 911 : simple, fabulous fixes for every fashion emergency / Joyce Corrigan.
p. cm.
Includes index.
ISBN 978-1-58816-871-9
1. Fashion design. 2. Fashion--Psychological aspects. 3. Women's clothing--Psychological aspects. I. Title.
TT507.C663 2012
746.9'2--dc23-
2011018795

10 9 8 7 6 5 4 3 2 1

marieclaire.com

For information about custom editions, special sales, premium and corporate purchases, please contact Sterling Special Sales Department at 800-805-5489 or specialsales@sterlingpublishing.com.

Distributed in Canada by Sterling Publishing
c/o Canadian Manda Group, 165 Dufferin Street
Toronto, Ontario, Canada M6K 3H6

Manufactured in China

Sterling ISBN 978-1-58816-871-9